THE CHARACTER BOOK:

A WORKBOOK TO ACCOMPANY

READ CHINESE

BOOK ONE

Timothy Light   Tao-chung Yao

Yale University

Copyright © by Far Eastern Publications, 1985. Printed in the United States of America by Lightning Source; Lavergne, Tennessee
All rights reserved. This book or its associated tapes may not be reproduced in whole or in part, in any form (except by reviewers for the public press), without written permission from the publisher.

ISBN- 10: 0-88710-137-2
ISBN- 13: 978-0-88710-137-3

This book is dedicated to our children:

Ann

Claire

James

in hopes that they will retain and develop their Chinese here in monolingual America.

CONTENTS

	Page
Preface	vii
Preliminary Lesson: Character Building	ix
Lesson I	1
Lesson II	10
Lesson III	23
Lesson IV	38
Lesson V	53
Review Lesson A	66
Lesson VI	77
Lesson VII	91
Lesson VIII	103
Lesson IX	114
Lesson X	127
Review Lesson B	140
Lesson XI	150
Lesson XII	163
Lesson XIII	175
Lesson XIV	187
Lesson XV	200
Review Lesson C	215
Lesson XVI	226
Lesson XVII	240
Lesson XVIII	254
Lesson XIX	267
Review Lesson D	277
Appendix I: Stroke Order List for Simplified Characters in *Read Chinese I*	289

PREFACE

This workbook is designed to accompany Fred Fang-yu Wang's famous and long-used Read Chinese Book I (RCI). RCI fully deserves its high reputation because it presents frequently used characters and combinations of characters in varied and interesting contexts. For thousands of Americans, RCI has been the gateway to happy and successful mastery of the recognition of Chinese characters.

Like most other texts, RCI is essentially a passive text. It requires the student to master the recognition of characters, but makes no demand for, and provides no opportunity for, the production of characters. It has been evident to many people that productive exercises are needed in the early stages of learning Chinese characters both in order to encourage productive use of characters, and to reinforce reading mastery. The Character Book aims to provide the demand and opportunity to produce characters.

In preparing this workbook, we feel we have perhaps broken a modest piece of ground, for, as far as we know, this is the first book devoted solely to enabling foreign students of Chinese to write words, sentences, and eventually simple discourse in Chinese. We have prepared this book because we sincerely believe that foreign students of Chinese--just like Chinese students of English--should expect (and be expected) to write Chinese at a level commensurate with their oral and receptive skills in Chinese. We believe that passive mastery of Chinese is no longer sufficient for the demands and opportunities that foreigners face in today's Chinese society. We believe that American and other foreign students are just as able to learn to write Chinese at a level commensurate with their overall achievement as are students of any other language. We further believe that today's students of Chinese begin the study of this language in the hope that they will learn to write it as well as speak and read it. In our experience, providing students with opportunities to write at their own level from the outset of their instruction leads to the habit and the expectation that they will as a matter of course maintain throughout

their Chinese training, so that they will quickly reach a
level of attainment which exceeds that of the non-native of
this book's two authors and others like him who were trained
in a time when it was unhappily assumed that foreigners
should not be asked to learn to write Chinese.

However, even in making this very modest claim, let us
note at the outset that our principal hope with this book is
that it will prompt others to derive more imaginative ways
of encouraging students to master all four skills in
Chinese. We are very much aware of the limited nature of
what we have to offer here and hope only that it might
(until superior products appear) stand as a symbol for the
belief that foreign learners of Chinese should and can
learn all four skills of the language.

***

In preparing this book we have been aided and encour-
aged by many people. Madeline Chu copied out the earliest
chapters. Timothy Wong read and commented on an early version. During several years when we taught together at the
University of Arizona, our students patiently worked through
the exercises then being written and made valuable comments
on them. Lu Jianji most carefully read the penultimate
manuscript and made scores of helpful corrections. The
final version was prepared for publication by Nikki Bado
(English), Gloria Lei, Wallace Sergent, Han Yuan, and Chou
Shizhen (Chinese). To all these people we express our
sincere thanks and at the same time gratefully let them off
the hook for any errors we may have committed.

***

All collaborations begin somewhere and have a sequence which
sooner or later gets asked about. For the record, and to
forestall inevitable questions: Lessons I-XVI were originally drafted by Light. Lesson XVII-Review Lesson D were
originally drafted by Yao. Each of us has worked on the
other's material extensively.

Timothy Light
Tao-chung Yao

THE CHARACTER BOOK

Preliminary Lesson: Character Building

1. <u>Chinese Writing</u>

   Chinese writing is the most intriguing way of writing in today's world. Although Chinese characters have changed greatly in form since their first invention, the present shapes retain direct links to scratches on stones and bones of thirty-five hundred years ago. Not only is their link to antiquity--and to man's first methods of writing via a kind of pictorial representation--a fascinating subject, but the persistence of Chinese writing in today's world remains intriguing. Chinese is the only language today that is written in a <u>logographic</u> script. All other contemporary systems of writing are sound-based. To modern eyes, it often seems that written Chinese, with its many symbols and difficult-to-master system is a cumbersome and outmoded tool that is a hindrance to modern development. Yet, not only is Chinese writing unique in its antiquity, and singular in form, it is unique as well in being the writing that is used by more people than any other single written language. Thus, as a student of Chinese, you are beginning to join the world's largest group of literate people!

   Through her long history, China has developed a highly refined and much prized art of writing. Calligraphy, the art of beautiful handwriting, stands as an equal to painting in China. Great calligraphers are honored and their works have been treasured throughout the ages, often preserved by being copied in stone. Even ordinary Chinese writing by ordinary people is a pleasure to behold. Bad, unsightly, careless writing is a rarity in China. School children are simply not permitted to write sloppily, and careless handwriting is considered a sign of ignorance and lack of education. Often to American eyes, the skills of Chinese calligraphy appear to be an inimitable achievement of miracle. This is not to say that there are not good American and other foreign writers of Chinese. There are, and many first-year students of Chinese in the United States develop a rather handsome hand after only brief practice. But for those to whom good handwriting does not come naturally even in English, a new skill must be learned as they learn Chinese.

That skill includes learning the correct formation of strokes, the ordering and arrangement of strokes, the proper number of strokes in each character, and the multi-stroke components that make up complex characters.

2. <u>Learning to Write Chinese</u>

The need for mastering the things that go into this skill is based not only on the obvious need for the foreign student of Chinese to appear educated to native users of Chinese, but there are practical reasons for mastering this skill as well. At the outset, it is useful to list them because they should be a part of every student's attitude toward the language he or she is learning:

1. Even though there are permissible variations in the ways that a few characters are written (for example the character 五 wǔ "five"), there is basically ONE RIGHT WAY to write each character. That way has been hallowed by tradition, and, whether it is ultimately the most efficient way to write or not (almost always it is), it is the right way, and foreign students will be judged by native speakers according to their mastery of that way.

2. The shapes of Chinese characters depend in many ways upon the order of strokes and how the strokes are formed. Although it is possible to write with the wrong order and the wrong stroke formation, more often than not, an <u>incorrectly written character</u> will <u>look incorrect</u> and have the same effect as an intelligible but misspelled word in English.

3. Chinese dictionaries and other lists of items depend in part on knowledge of stroke-count (how many strokes there are in a character), and sometimes on the order in which those strokes go. Moreover, the most common method of arranging words in a dictionary relies on multi-stroke components of characters. So knowledge of the makeup of characters is needed for effective use of language tools later on.

4. Phonetic "spelling" of characters is, of course, impossible in Chinese. But just like us in using English, users of Chinese often need to be able to tell each other orally how to write a character. Oral "spelling" is possible in Chinese. It is done by use of components of characters which have full meanings and pronunciations in their own right.

PRELIMINARY LESSON

> "Finger spelling" is also common in Chinese. One person may use his/her finger to write a character in the air or on another person's hand, and the other will catch the intended character from the stroke order and count even though the character itself, of course, cannot be seen. Once again, the user of Chinese cannot give or understand a spelling unless he or she knows the ways in which characters are built.

A fifth of the length of Read Chinese Book I is devoted to aids that will help you write characters correctly through learning the proper ordering of strokes and the number of strokes in each character. Even before beginning your study of Chinese, you should know what these aids are and where they are to be found. There are four of them, and they are found of pp. 170-206 of RCI. Turn to p. 170. There you will find a list of the 300 characters introduced in the book. The characters are arranged in columns according to the number of strokes in each character. Read down the first four columns (those on p. 170). How many characters have one stroke? How many have two? How many have 3, 4, 5, 6? Now turn to p. 175. There is a chart illustrating the basic stroke forms. The textbook of an attentive student will have this page dog-eared after first-year Chinese because he or she will refer back to it upon learning each new stroke type. Your teacher will demonstrate the formation of these strokes as he or she teaches. Later in this lesson, we will go over the most common ones in the numbers 1-10. The seven rules for stroke order given on p. 175 should be memorized. If they are memorized, they will become an automatic habit of your hand, and when you learn new characters in later years, you will find that you automatically copy out the new form correctly the first time.

Finally, beginning on p. 176 is a stroke order analysis for each of the 300 characters introduced in RCI. From your first writing of each character through your practice of all characters you should refer to this list. Each page contains ten characters arranged in two columns. The order is given by successive writings of parts of the characters building up to the full form. Later on, when complex characters are introduced, components of characters that are already familiar will be given as wholes, and you will be expected to know their stroke order from earlier exposure. The appendix to The Character Book contains the stroke order analysis for the simplified characters used in Read Chinese Book I.

3. <u>The Numbers 1-10</u>

The first ten characters introduced in <u>RCI</u> are the numbers 1-10. The Chinese numbers employ common strokes and illustrate most of the basic principles of stroke order and formation. They provide a good set to demonstrate how to proceed in learning to write Chinese correctly.

First turn to p. 175 and read through the seven rules of stroke order several times. If you can memorize them now, it will be helpful; if not, at least establish a familiarity with them. Now, turn to p. 177, and look at the character for "one" <u>yī</u> 一 . Its single stroke is horizontal. It is the simplest character in Chinese. But, just like the most complex one, it should be written so as to divide the space in a box evenly and esthetically. The "box" referred to is not just a metaphor. Instead of being lined, Chinese writing paper is squared off, and each square should be filled with one character. Here is a sample of normal Chinese writing paper. The squares in the stroke order list in <u>RCI</u> are based on traditional writing paper. You should do your own practice writing on such sheets.

PRELIMINARY LESSON

一	二	三	四	五	六	七	八	九	十		

Every character should "fill" the box assigned to it. "Fill" obviously does not mean "black out" or anything like it. "Fill" here means to use the space in a way that is pleasing to the eye and that is balanced. The single stroke for the character yī 一 is placed in the middle, evenly between the right and left sides of the box, and slightly above the middle of the vertical space. That is, there is less space above the character than below it. On squared paper, write several copies of the yī given in p. 177.

Èr 二 and sān 三 follow the same principles as yī. The top stroke of èr 二 is, of course, higher than the single stroke of yī 一, and the bottom stroke lower. The whole character is balanced between the right and left sides of the box, but there is more space below the character than above it; it is slightly higher than vertical center. The top stroke of èr is shorter than the bottom stroke, though it, too, is centered horizontally. Sān is centered in the same fashion. The shortest stroke is the middle one, and the top is second shortest.

Yī 一 èr 二 sān 三 all illustrate principles two and three of stroke and order, that is, characters are written from left to right and from top to bottom. These two principles are the keys to remember in all circumstances. All the other rules are variations of these principles, where the shape of strokes does not allow for an obvious left-right, top-bottom movement.

Sz̀ 四 illustrates principles one and four. Where there are corners, the beginning is the upper left hand corner, with the vertical stroke first. Where there is a "box" enclosing another part of a character, the left side (one stroke) and the top and right side (together one stroke) are written first. Then the material for the inside is written, and finally, the bottom horizontal line closes off the whole.

Now write twenty each of the numbers one through four.

一 二 三 四

Wǔ 五 is the first character that seems to violate a principle. The first and second strokes seem to fit the pattern of top to bottom, but the third stroke seems to put a horizontal line after the vertical that cuts it (rule five):

The reason for the ordering may be because the horizontal stroke is not simply a horizontal line, but basically the same stroke that makes the top and right side of the box in sz̀ 四 . Whatever the reason, native speakers of Chinese actually disagree on the ordering of this character, and some write it like this:

This variation among native writers is pointed out at the outset so that you will not become disillusioned when you discover it on your own. For a small percentage of characters, where the rules are ambiguous, there is disagreement among Chinese writers of Chinese. That disagreement over a small number of characters should not be the cause for a foreign student concluding that any old way is all right. Any old way is not all right, and even when there is disagreement over a stroke or two, there are usually only two ways to write the character and no more. The room for initiative and eccentricity is very slight indeed. As was said above, basically there is ONLY ONE RIGHT WAY.

Liù 六 and chī 七 reflect rules one, two, three, and five perfectly. Now write twenty each of numbers five through seven.

Bā 八 reflects rule two.

Jyǒu 九 reflects the basic principle of rule one; though it appears to have the same problem as wǔ 五 . There is no variation in the way that native speakers write the character.

Shŕ 十 aptly illustrates rule five; the horizontal is written before the vertical line cutting it.

Now write twenty each of numbers eight through ten.

4. The Remaining Characters of Lesson One: An Exercise

   You should now work through the remaining characters of lesson one in the same fashion as you have been guided through the numbers. As an aid, do the following exercise as you study.

   For each chapter, identify and write the number of the rules of stroke order being applied in the stroke order models on pp. 178 and 179. For each character write one very large copy of which you write the order-numbers of the strokes, as is done in the six examples given on p. 176, and as is done below for yuè 月 :

   yuè 月   month, moon

Rules 1, 2, 3, 4.

   Finally, for each character, write twenty samples on squared paper.

5. The Learning of Chinese Characters: By Natives and Foreigners

   Chinese children learn to write their own language by the diligent copying of each new character tens or even hundreds of times. Their classroom instruction consists of teachers explaining stroke and component order and then of him or her requiring the pupils to master (totally!) both the characters and the explanations given. Chinese classrooms have a great deal of recitation, both choral and individual. Pupils are required to be able to "spell" characters they have learned by naming the strokes in correct order and by naming the components of complex characters in correct order. First-grade children in the People's Republic of China learn between six hundred and eight hundred characters. Second graders learn about the same; and in each of the remaining years of elementary school, children learn about five hundred characters. A child, therefore, will have an active written vocabulary of over three thousand characters by the time he or she leaves elementary school.

It would be nice if foreigners could learn any language with the <u>apparent</u> unconsciousness of the children who speak that language natively. Unfortunately, adults do not learn anything the way children do, and the pious hope that a little injection of childhood would make language learning miraculously easy is doomed to disillusionment. In the learning of written Chinese there are a few special reasons why foreign learners will not want to imitate Chinese children. Like foreign students of Chinese, Chinese children beginning to write their own language are learning the world's most unsystematic and difficult writing system. But, unlike those foreigners, the children already know the <u>language</u>. What children learn is limited to mastering the symbols that are used to represent on paper something they already know. The foreigner learning Chinese is learning both the spoken language and the new symbolic system and the differences between the two all at the same time. Obviously, the foreigner's job is much more difficult. The child has six years of elementary school to attain a level of basic literate fluency. Adults generally do not have that kind of time to master a writing system. Because of difficulty and because of time constraints, corners must be cut to make the foreigner's task less arduous than it otherwise would be. Corners are cut chiefly by limiting the number of characters required of foreign learners to those that are of known high frequency and that are frequent in the kind of materials which adults will read (as opposed to children's reading material, which may include among its most frequent vocabulary items such words as the names of animals, familiar kinship terms, etc.). Many of the items that are prevalent in children's vocabularies (in all languages) are very rare among adults, and these items are not worth learning early on even in an alphabetically written language, to say nothing of Chinese. What you are asked to learn in the first two or three years of Chinese study, therefore, is a bare-boned, skeletal vocabulary that will enable you to read the vast majority of the characters (usually up to 85 or 90 percent) on any given page of adult Chinese. After you have mastered these, you will find branching out into specialized areas much easier.

For the native-speaking child, new characters are more often than not simply graphic representations of sounds whose meaning he or she already knows. Recalling such items is not difficult, because they fit into an already mastered pattern of language. For the foreigner, the graphic symbol

is learned together with the sound it represents and with
the meaning that both represent. Because there is this
three-way tie (graphic-phonetic-semantic: i.e. character-
pronunciation-meaning) that must be learned, students are
strongly urged to prepare vocabulary cards as an aid to
learning. Many teachers require this and check the cards
for each lesson to be sure that the characters are written
correctly. Even if not required by your teacher, vocabulary
cards should be prepared because cards that can be sorted in
an infinite number of ways provide the surest way to learn
and test your mastery of shapes and sounds and meanings.

6. <u>Character Cards</u>

Here is a suggested format for character cards:

On the first side, write the character large. Write it
neatly so that in subsequent copying and study of the character you will be looking at a correct version of it. Many
students like to write their character cards in felt pen or
thick-stroke fountain pens. A few even use traditional
Chinese brush-pens for this purpose. Certainly, the more
artistic pleasure you get from preparing the cards, the
easier it will be to learn the characters written on the
cards. It is suggested that you leave some room at the
bottom of the card to write (small, of course,) cursive
versions of the characters, when you learn them, and the
base radicals of the characters when you learn those.

<u>Side One</u>

On the second side, put the pronunciation and English
meaning of the single character at the top and then follow
it with the "combinations" (usually words) of more than one
character that you learn.

<u>Side Two</u>

rén　person
大人　adult
中國人　Chinese person
人人　everyone
好人　good person
女人　woman

PRELIMINARY LESSON   xix

A character component is a single part of a character
which by itself forms a character or an element with pronunciation or meaning. In the character tā 他 "he, she,
it," the left hand portion is rén 人 "person", and the
right hand portion is yě 也 "also." The left hand portion
of this character is called the <u>radical</u> and indicates that
the character has something to do with humans. The right
hand portion on this character is called the <u>phonetic</u>
component because in its older pronunciation *i̯ad̯ it was
pronounced the same as the full character 也 minus the
radical consonant *di̯a. A very large number of characters
are made up of a radical and a phonetic. As you learn more
characters, you will find the radicals and phonetics
becoming familiar to you and you will find that you
automatically begin to think of characters as made up of
various components. As an example, look at the character
<u>ting</u>, "listen."

Although it seems complicated at the outset, this character
will prove to be an easy one to remember when you have
learned it; because it is made up of recurrent parts:

<u>ěr</u> "ear" 耳   <u>wang</u> "king" 王   <u>shŕ</u> "ten" 十

<u>yī</u> "one" 一   <u>syīn</u> "heart" 心

The componential buildup of characters is an important
thing to learn because it will enable you to learn new characters more easily. Particularly important are the radicals
because dictionaries are organized according to radicals and
stroke count. In this workbook you will only be asked to
identify components and similar portions of characters.
There will be no formal training at this stage in the traditional components that make up characters because the
authors feel that you have enough to learn as it is right
now. Nevertheless, try to notice similar parts among characters as you proceed in your learning. From this you will
learn the componential build up of characters automatically
and in later stages your learning of the components will be
made more formal.

7. How to Use The Character Book

The purpose of this book is to provide extensive opportunities for you to write Chinese. The authors feel that writing is important both for its own sake and as an aid to efficient reading. Nowadays, more and more foreign learners of Chinese are called upon to be able to write grammatically acceptable Chinese. Even if one does not need to be able to write extended discourses in Chinese, practice in writing inevitably aids in learning to read, for you can certainly read easily anything you can write fluently. Following the development of RCI, this workbook begins with simple copying of exercises for simple characters. Very soon, however, you are asked to write full sentences, and well before the end of the book you are asked to make up whole paragraphs of your own on set topics. We hope that this gradual introduction to Chinese writing will prepare you for further work in writing so that after you have studied two or three years of Chinese you will be able to correspond in simple Chinese, fill out forms in Chinese and write simple essays in Chinese.

We offer these simple pointers to aid you in using the book.

1) Where blanks are given in an exercise, work quickly, and fill in the blank in this copy of this book.

2) Where blanks are not provided, we have spaced many of the exercises so that you can write your answer in the book if you wish. But we suggest that you not do this, rather, it will be more beneficial if you write your exercises on separate sheets of paper.

3) There are more exercises in this book than any teacher will want to assign, and we do not encourage teachers to assign all of them. We do, however, encourage students to do all the exercises because the practice will give them the opportunity they need to truly master the written form of the Chinese that they have learned up to now.

4) Good luck, and have fun!!!

PRELIMINARY LESSON

P.S.: An answer key containing answers to some of the exercises in the workbook is available separately. It is called The Character Book Answer Key and is available from

FAR EASTERN PUBLICATIONS
YALE UNIVERSITY
340 EDWARDS STREET BOX 2505A
NEW HAVEN, CONNECTICUT 06520
(203) 436-1075

THE CHARACTER BOOK
LESSON I

A. Exercises on Character Meaning and Use

Ex. 1: Write the Chinese numbers from 1 to 10

Ex. 2: In the blanks, write the English equivalents for the following numbers.

四____ 九____ 三____ 五____ 十____

七____ 六____ 八____ 一____ 二____

八十三____ 九十____ 十六____

三十七____ 四十五____ 十五____

二十____ 七十三____ 三十七____

八十二____ 二十九____ 六十五____

七十四____ 十六____ 六十七____

二十二____ 九十九____ 五十九____

THE CHARACTER BOOK

Ex. 3: In the blanks, write the Chinese equivalents of the English numbers.

1_____ 9_____ 10_____ 6_____ 2_____

8_____ 3_____ 11_____ 7_____ 5_____

33_____ 48_____ 89_____ 16_____

76_____ 62_____ 32_____ 24_____

85_____ 52_____ 29_____ 99_____

13_____ 77_____ 30_____ 21_____

46_____ 65_____ 82_____ 44_____

Ex. 4: Continue each series of numbers for as many numbers as there are blanks. One example is given.

a) 十，二十，三十，<u>四十</u>，<u>五十</u>，<u>六十</u>，<u>七十</u>，<u>八十</u>，<u>九十</u>．

b) 三，六，九，_____，_____，_____，_____，_____，_____，_____．

c) 七，十四，二十一，_____，_____，_____，_____．

d) 四，九，十五，二十二，_____，_____，_____，_____，_____．

e) 四，十，十六，_____，_____，_____，_____，_____，_____．

LESSON I   3

Ex. 5: Draw lines connecting the Chinese and English
        equivalents. One example is given.

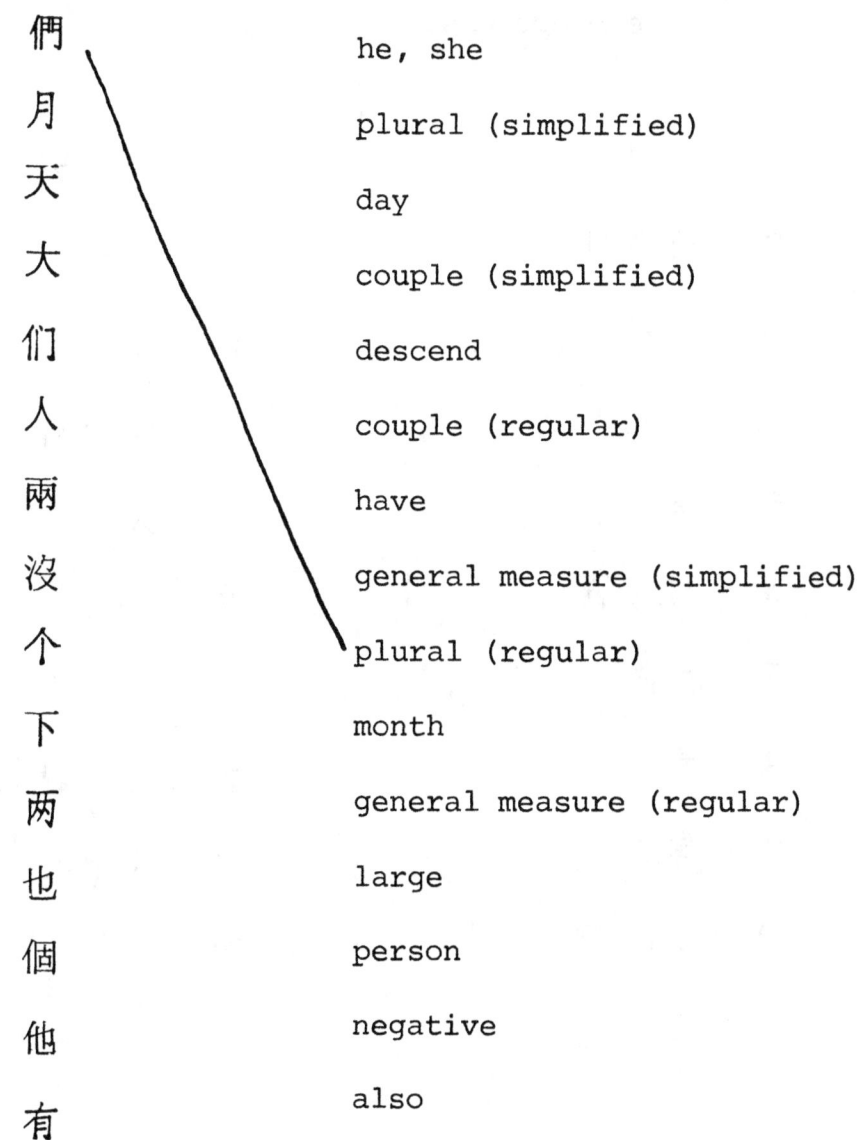

Ex. 6: Provide Yale Romanization for the following expressions:

1. 二月
2. 三個月
3. 上月
4. 九個人
5. 有一天
6. 七八個
7. 我們
8. 是不是
9. 有的
10. 他們的
11. 兩三天
12. 小的
13. 不大
14. 你也有
15. 大人
16. 四月
17. 六七十
18. 五六個人
19. 四十四
20. 下月

LESSON I   5

Ex. 7:   Put the letter of the English equivalent in the
         blank beside the appropriate Chinese expression.
         One example is given.

         我   __f__   a. next month
         是   _____   b. they, them
         下月   _____   c. China
         大人   _____   d. is, am, are
         一個人 _____   e. two days
         沒有   _____   f. I, me
         你的   _____   g. one person
         兩天   _____   h. adult
         中 gwo _____   i. have not
         他們   _____   j. yours

Ex. 8:   In the blanks, write the English equivalent for
         each Chinese expression.

         沒有 _____   他的 _____   我們的 _____

         不是 _____   小 háidz _____   兩個月 _____

         上 syīngchī _____   天天 _____   十二月 _____

         三個月 _____   下 chē _____   有 chyán _____

         你的 _____   jǐ 个人 _____   是 _____

         他们 _____   兩个人 _____   兩天 _____

Ex. 9: In the blanks, write the Chinese equivalent for each English expression.

my, mine	_____	4 adults	_____
also	_____	next month	_____
miss	_____	we (simplified)	_____
33 people	_____	ascend	_____
our, ours	_____	2-3 days	_____
board a ship	_____	16 months	_____
they, them	_____	evening	_____
there is not	_____	wealthy	_____
everyone	_____	2 months (simplified)	_____

B. Exercises on Character Shape and Origin

Ex. 10: In each group, circle the characters which begin in handwriting with the same stroke as the characters already circled.

a ⊙一 六 十 人 也 有 我 天 大

b ⊙人 個 大 九 你 有 們 是 不

c ⊙我 沒 的 小 中 六

LESSON I   7

Ex. 11: SEEK AND FIND. Inside the box are thirty-six
         characters, including the 12 given below the
         box. Find those 12, circle them, and put the
         letters beside them in the circle. Two examples
         are given.

入	犬	找	你	的	少
他	目	不	大	下	力
沒	門	是	也	日	白
九	(b)月	走	夫	們	耳
太	住	天	行	明	(a)八
問	小	以	友	半	出

a 八   b 月   c 沒   d 下   e 們   f 也

g 不   h 小   i 的   j 是   k 九   l 天

C. Review Exercises

Ex. 12: For each set of sentences select the correct character(s) from those given above the set, and write them in the blanks to make good sentences.

A 中 也 是 你 他 下 上

1. 他 ___ ___ gwo 人。

2. ___ 有，我 ___ 有。

3. ___ 月 ___ 沒 chyán，___ 月 ___ 沒 chyán。

B 小 不 們 的 個 大 是

1. 我 ___ shū ___ hǎu？

2. 他 ___ 兩 ___ 人沒 chyán。

3. ___ 的是我 ___。___ 的 ___ 你 ___。

LESSON I

Ex. 13: Translate the following into English.

1. 他們是 hǎu péngyou。

2. 你們是中 gwo 人。

3. 我沒有 chyán。

4. 他 上月沒 chyán。

5. 我們也不是中 gwo 人。

Ex. 14: Rewrite the following expressions, replacing simplified characters for full characters, and vice versa.

1. 他們   2. 兩個人

3. 两个月   4. 我们

THE CHARACTER BOOK

LESSON II

A. Exercises on Character Meaning and Use

Ex. 1: Draw lines connecting the Chinese and English equivalents. One example is given.

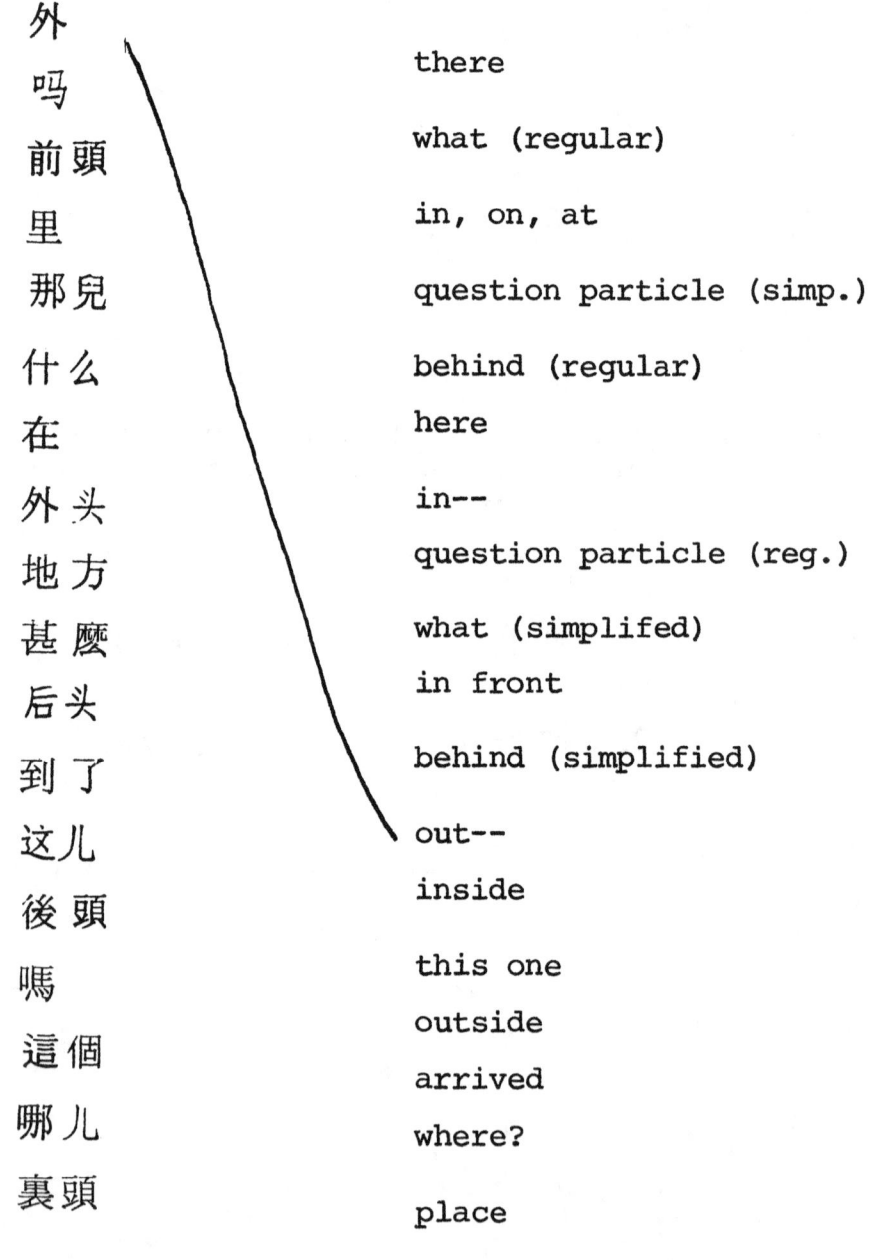

Ex. 2: Give Yale Romanizations for the following expressions.

1. 地方
2. 沒甚麼
3. 裏頭
4. 這個人
5. 到了
6. 那兒
7. 外頭
8. 前頭
9. 後頭
10. 上頭
11. 在這兒
12. 在下頭
13. 那個人
14. 在前頭
15. 在甚麼地方
16. 哪兒？
17. 在嗎？

Ex. 3: Put the letter of the English equivalent in the blank beside the appropriate Chinese expression. One example is given.

這兒 ___g___   a. already arrived
lái 了 _____   b. that person
那個人 _____   c. outside
裏頭 _____   d. there
地方 _____   e. what
甚麼 _____   f. have come
在 _____   g. here
那兒 _____   h. place
外頭 _____   i. in, at, on
                 j. inside
yǐjing 到了_____

Ex. 4: Fill in the blanks with characters which make a correct expression. Use the characters at the top. One example is given.

我，七，天，前，外，方，個，在，
甚，十，地，到，有，兒，麼。

這__地__   那__
__了   __頭
甚__   __方
__這兒   沒__
__們   六__人

LESSON II   13

Ex. 5: The characters in each of the groups below do not
        make complete expressions by themselves. For each
        group one other character is needed. Write that
        character in beside each character in each group and,
        on the line below, the meaning of the expression
        you have made. One example is given.

a   那兒   這兒   哪兒
     ___there___ ___here___   ___where___

b   那___   這___   哪___
     _____   _____   _____

c   後___   外___   前___   裏___
     _____   _____   _____   _____

d   我___   你___   他___
     _____   _____   _____

e   我___   你___   他___
     _____   _____   _____

Ex. 6: In the blanks write the English equivalents of
        the Chinese expressions.

到了_____   兒 dz _____   那個_____

這兒_____   这个_____   前頭_____

甚麼?_____   外頭_____   在_____

裏頭_____   到中 gwò chyù_____ 什么_____

地方_____   後頭_____   里头_____

Ex. 7: For each set of sentences and phrases select the correct character(s) given above the set and write them in the blanks to make good sentences or phrases.

A   個 兒 那 這 在 哪

1. ___ ___ 人 ____ 後 頭。

2. 他 在 ____ ____ 。

3. 他 們 ____ 前 頭。

4. 中 gwo ____ ____ ____ ?

B   的 前 頭 們 個

1. 我 ____ shū 。

2. 他 ____ 兩 ____ 人。

3. ___ ___ 那 個 人。

4. 我 們 在 ____ ____ 。

C   地 到 外 在 裏 方 了 頭

1. 他 不 ___ ___ 頭。 他 ____ ____ ____ 。

2. 他 ____ 甚 麼 ____ ____ ?

3. 這 是 甚 麼 ____ ____ ?

4. 他 們 yǐjing ____ ____ 。

LESSON II   15

Ex. 8: Translate the following into English.

1. 那是甚麼？

2. 他在那兒。

3. 他在哪兒？

4. 我們在外頭。

5. 他的 shū 在前頭。

6. 你們在甚麼地方？

7. 這是甚麼地方？

8. 裏頭那個人...

9. 後頭那個人...

10. 到了中 gwo ...

11. 那個是我的。

12. 這個是他的。

13. 小的在哪兒？

14. 大的在甚麼地方？

15. 那是我的。

Ex. 9: Translate the following into Chinese.

1. What place?

2. this person

3. that person

4. Which person?

5. They have already arrived.

6. We are in the back.

7. They are inside.

8. the person (who is) in front . . .

9. the person (who is) in back . . .

10. this place

11. that place

12. They are in that place.

13. She is not on top.

14. We're not outside.

15. He is not there.

LESSON II   17

                     B.   Exercises on the Story

Ex. 10:   Complete the sentences by copying the correct
          characters from the story. Sentences included here
          skip some of what is in the book.

1. 我 gēn 我 tàitai shwō: "Jīn 天 ___ ___ chī

    ___ ___ fàn?

2. 他說 : "Pùdz ___ ___ ___ ___ ___ ___ hǎu tsài."

3. " 我 syǎng, jīn ___ ___ ___ ___ ___ ___ chyù chī

    fàn chyù ba."

4. 我 ___ ___ ___ ___ háidz gēn ___ ___ ___

    kwài ___ chūchyu ___.

5. Háidz ___ ___ ___ ___ ___ dzǒu, ___ tàitai gēn ___

    ___ ___ ___.

6. ___ ___ shŕhou tsúng ___ ___ lái ___ ___ ___

    lǎutàitai.

7. ___ ___ byé ___, ___ ___ tàitai ___ mǔchin.

8. "___ ___ ___ ___ jyā chyù ___. ___ ___ dōu

    ___ ___ jyā, ___ syǎng ___ ___ ___ dìng ___

    ___ ___, swóyi ___ ___ ___ ___ lái ___."

Ex. 11:   Questions on the Story.

1. Shéi gēn 我 tàitai shwō. "Jīn 天 我們 chr̄ 甚麼 fàn?
2. Jīn 天 dzǎu 上 我 tàitai mǎi tsài 沒有?
3. 我 tàitai syǎng 在 哪兒 chr̄ fàn?
4. 他 syǎng 到 哪個 fàngwǎn兒 chyù chr̄ fàn chyù?
5. Shéi 在 前頭 dzǒu? Shéi 在 後頭?
6. 他們 在 fàngwǎn兒 裏 dzwò 下了。那個 shŕhou shéi tsúng 外頭, lái 了?
7. 我 tàitai 的 mǔchīn shwō 甚麼?
8. 我 tàitai 的 mǔchīn ài shwōhwà 嗎?
9. 我 tàitai 的 mǔchīn shwō 的 hwà 沒有 甚麼?
10. 我 shwō 甚麼?

LESSON II

C. Exercises on Character Shape and Origin

Ex 12: In each group, circle the characters which begin in handwriting with the same stroke, as in the characters circled.

a   ⓔ在   前   甚   頭   兒   了   七   六

b   ⓜ麼   地   方   這   到   裏   外   前

c   ⓒ後   你   那   們   外   他   中   個

Ex. 13: In each of the groups below the characters share one similar part. Circle that part in each character. One example is given.

a   ⓜ月   ⓐ有

b   一   天   七   十

c   人   個   你   們   大

d   在   地

e   地   他   也

D. Review Exercises

Ex. 14: SEEK AND FIND. Inside the box there are 36 characters, including the 12 given below the box. Find those 12, circle them, and put the letters beside them in the circle. One example is given.

了	豆	九	外	兒	甚
子	頭ⓐ	衣	上	個	日
候	我	裏	有	月	走
後	至	存	沒	那	這
行	到	的	是	大	地
房	方	少	前	天	也

a 頭　b 裏　c 前　d 那　e 這　f 了

g 到　h 地　i 兒　j 外　k 後　l 方

LESSON II

Ex. 15 : SCRAMBLE. Snaking its way through the jumble of characters in the box below is the Chinese for "Where is he? Is he outside? Is he inside? Is he in front? Is he in back? He is not outside. He is not inside. He is not in front. He is not in back. He is here." Draw a line connecting the characters that make up these sentences. Remember, they are all joined, but may go in any direction, and there is no punctuation.

能	沒	你	本	不	十	先	生	用	後	吃	六	沒	十	他
回	有	在	在	四	他	了	很	都	時	飯	七	有	在	我
可	錢	後	個	有	九	頭	少	對	作	請	月	來	九	哪
以	頭	是	我	到	他	子	前	嗎	來	坐	兩	去	的	兒
他	很	那	們	頭	個	不	在	他	頭	問	人	買	他	也
在	會	兒	在	裏	月	兒	多	在	裏	能	天	在	你	上
麼	這	麼	不	頭	麼	這	前	些	西	在	外	賣	也	下
兒	說	不	他	上	什	頭	話	他	他	頭	大	是	們	頭
五	話	是	頭	月	方	後	嗎	是	嗎	會	中	那	在	到
四	中	外	外	日	頭	後	在	他	字	日	國	兒	麼	了
九	日	國	在	嗎	地	前	說	外	寫	回	個	是	方	兒
他	都	他	不	他	外	上	來	兒	可	以	兒	這	什	這

Ex. 16: Rewrite the following expressions, replacing simplified characters with full characters, and vice versa.

1. 甚麼： _____

2. 裏頭： _____

3. 你 hǎu 嗎？ _____

4. 後頭： _____

5. 在这儿 _____

6. 什么 _____

THE CHARACTER BOOK

LESSON III

A. Exercises on Character Meaning and Use

Ex. 1: Draw lines connecting the Chinese and English equivalents.

先生	Chinese language
说话	Chinese people
很多	beautiful
中国人	quite a few
很不少	to speak (regular)
给他	to speak (simplified)
到這兒來	sir, mister, husband
下去	go down
去	to come
兒子	very many, much
他要	come here
說話	give him
好看	son
中國話	to go

Ex. 2: Give Yale Romanizations for the following expressions.

1. 你好嗎？

2. 說話

3. 中國人

4. 到外國去

5. 兒子

6. 下去

7. 上來

8. 給他

9. 先生

10. 多少

11. 很好看

12. 外國話

13. 他不要

14. 好了

15. 看一看

LESSON III   25

Ex. 3: Put the letter of the English equivalent in the
       blank beside the appropriate Chinese expression.

yǐ 子 _____   a. be well again; it's already
                            done
sywé 生 _____
                        b. foreign language
不多 _____
                        c. chair
很好看 _____
                        d. take a look
給他一個 _____
                        e. speak Chinese
說中國話 _____
                        f. not many/much
好不好？_____
                        g. student
看看 _____
                        h. very beautiful
外國話 _____
                        i. How about it?
好了 _____
                        j. Give him/her one.

Ex. 4: In the blanks, write the English equivalents of the following Chinese expressions.

先生 _____ 很多 _____ 多少？_____

很不少 _____ 很少 _____ 很好 _____

好看 _____ 好不好？_____ 好了 _____

看看 _____ 看 shū _____ 說話 _____

tīng 說 _____ 說 gùshr _____ 中國話 _____

中國人 _____ 外國 _____ 外國話 _____

小 hái 子 _____ yǐ 子 _____ 要 _____

他不去 _____ 上來 _____ 下來 _____

到這兒來 _____ 到外國去 _____

給我 _____ 給他 _____

LESSON III

Ex. 5: In the blanks, give the Chinese equivalents for the English expressions.

go abroad_____ come up_____ child_____

important_____ went_____ give him_____

beautiful_____ talk_____ student_____

read a book_____ Chinese language_____

How about it?_____ how much, many?_____

sir, teacher_____ you first_____

quite a few_____ very good, well_____

talk (simplified)_____ China (simplified)_____

Ex. 6: In the space beside each character write a character which has an opposite or approximately opposite meaining.

去 _____　　　前 _____　　　後 _____

上 _____　　　外 _____　　　那 _____

裏 _____　　　小 _____　　　下 _____

Ex. 7: In the blank beside each character, write in a character which forms a proper combination and give the meaning of the combination.

a 上 _____ _____　　　f 多 _____ _____

b 說 _____ _____　　　g 先 _____ _____

c 好 _____ _____　　　h 不 _____ _____

d 看 _____ _____　　　i 兒 _____ _____

e 中 _____ _____　　　j 好 _____ _____

LESSON III   29

Ex. 8: For each set of sentences and phrases, select the
       correct character(s) given above the set and write
       them in the blanks to make good sentences or
       phrases.

A   去   給   國   來   到

  1. 我不＿＿外＿＿ ＿＿ 。

  2. ＿＿這兒＿＿＿ 。

  3. ＿＿我一 kwài táng 。

  4. 我不＿＿中＿＿＿ 。

B   個   說   那   中   很   人   國

  1. ＿＿＿＿人＿＿好看 。

  2. 他的兒子＿＿ ＿＿國話 。

  3. ＿＿ ＿＿人是＿＿國＿＿ 。

  4. 他是＿＿ ＿＿人 。

C   生   中   那   看   先   國

  1. 你＿＿ ＿＿是＿＿國人 。

  2. 那個中國＿＿＿＿說＿＿＿＿話 。

  3. 你＿＿＿ dzǒu 。

  4. ＿＿個 sywé ＿＿＿＿很好＿＿＿＿ 。

Ex. 9: Translate the following into English.

1. 他要我先去。

2. 你的兒子很好看。

3. 這兒的中國人不少。

4. 你們不說中國話嗎?

5. 我們的先生是 Dé 國人。

6. 你們有多少 sywé 生?

7. 那兒的 Fà 國人很多

8. 我給他兩 kwài táng 。

9. 中國 sywé 生很好看。

10. 他們有兩個兒子。

LESSON III

Ex. 10: Translate the following into Chinese.
(write simplified characters)

1. He is not coming.

2. Will they go?

3. I'll take a look first.

4. The teacher's not coming.

5. She is very good looking.

6. I'll give her three of them.

7. What does their son want?

8. We speak Chinese there.

9. That person is German.

10. He is going abroad.

Ex. 11: SEEK AND FIND. Inside the box there are 36 characters, including the 12 whose English meanings are given below. Find those 12, circle them, and put the letter of the character in the circle.

有	合	少	大	女	來
月	給	七	小	子	到
我	塔	你	去	兒	很
看	說	生	上	右	娘
日	多	話	裏	好	圓
友	外	先	人	在	國

a. go   b. country   c. give   d. come   e. good
f. look g. much   h. first i. few   j. very
k. small l. speak

LESSON III   33

        B. Exercises on the Story

Ex. 12: Complete the following sentences by copying the appropriate characters from the story.

1. Jāng ____ ____ wèn: 「____ ____ chyán ne?」

2. Lǐ ____ ____ ____: 「Yú ____ ____ ____ ____ ____, ____ ____ néng ____ chyán。」

3. Lǐ ____ ____ ____: 「好！ ____ ____。」

4. ____ tīng ____ ____ ____ É ____ pù 子 ____ ____ ____ ____ ____ Dé ____ fàngwǎn 兒。」

5. 到 ____ ____ 去， ____ ____ ____ ?

6. ____ ____ ____ fàngwǎn 兒 ____ ____, Jāng ____ ____ ____ ____ ____ ____ yú。

7. Yú ____ ____, Jāng ____ ____ ____ ____ ____, gēn Lǐ ____ ____ ____: 「____ ____ syǎng chr̄, ____ chr̄ ba。」

Ex. 13: Questions on the Story.

1. Jāng 先生 gēn Lǐ 先生說甚麼？
2. Lǐ 先生問 Jāng 先生甚麼？
3. 他們到哪個飯 gwǎn 兒去？
4. Dé 國飯 gwǎn 兒在哪兒？
5. Jāng 先生要了甚麼？
6. Lǐ 先生要了甚麼？
7. Shéi 吃了 yú ？
8. 飯 gwǎn 兒裏的 Dé 國人 yùng 哪國話 gēn Lǐ 先生說：「Nín hái 沒給 chyán ne。」
9. Lǐ 先生爲甚麼不給 chyán ？
10. Jāng 先生問那個 Dé 國人甚麼？

LESSON III

C. Exercises on Character Shape and Origin

Ex. 14: In each group below, the characters share one similar part. Circle that part in each group. One example is given.

a (彳)艮 (彳)後

b 要 好 女

c 小 少 你

d 他 來 們 你 大

e 來 天 不 下 一

f 說 話 這

g 國 我

h 他 地 也

Ex. 15: In each group below, circle the characters which begin with the same stroke in handwriting as the ones circled.

a 來 去 看 說 好 (到)

b 小 是 你 (少) 上 十

c 的 也 (我) 先 沒 生

d 方 兒 麼 來 這 (話)

D. Review Exercises

Ex. 16: Select characters from Column B which have the opposite meaning to those in Column A and write them beside their opposites.

A 小____ 上____   B 下   去

　　裏____ 少____   多   後

　　前____ 來____   外   大

Ex. 17: Translate into Chinese.

1. Are you a foreigner?

2. He does not speak Chinese.

3. She is very good looking.

4. How many do you want.

5. They are inside.

6. There are a lot of adults outside.

7. What is that thing of yours?

8. How much do they want?

9. That gentleman is not coming here.

10. They don't give me.

LESSON III

Ex. 18: Rewrite the following expressions, replacing simplified characters with full characters, and vice versa.

1. 说话 : _____

2. 中国人 : _____

3. 给我 : _____

4. 上來 : _____

5. 說中國話 _____

THE CHARACTER BOOK

LESSON IV

A. Exercises on Character Meaning and Use

Ex. 1: Draw lines connecting the Chinese and English equivalents.

	buy (regular)
用	wish to
東	buy (simplified)
這 些	time
賣	sell (simplified)
钱	but
西	correct
买	use
作	
時 候	east
卖	these
錢	money (regular)
对	sell (regular)
都 好	do
可 是	money (simplified)
想	west
買	all are well

38

LESSON IV

Ex. 2: Give Yale Romanization for the following expressions.

1. 作事

2. 有錢

3. 時候

4. 買東西

5. 想一想

6. 對了

7. 可是

8. 那些

9. 有用

10. 作買賣

11. 不用

12. 都不去

13. 不對

14. 好些人

15. 沒用

Ex. 3: Put the letter of the English equivalent in the blank beside the appropriate Chinese expression.

對了 _____   a. be rich

東 _____   b. thing

買 _____   c. correct

事 _____   d. a good many people

不用 _____   e. east

東西 _____   f. business

想想 _____   g. buy

好些人 _____ h. no use to

有錢 _____   i. think over

沒用 _____   j. useless

LESSON IV

Ex. 4: In the blanks, write the English equivalents of the following Chinese expressions.

可 yǐ _____ 不對 _____ 買東西 _____

賣 _____ 作事 _____ 沒錢 _____

時候 _____ 買賣 _____ 有錢 _____

作買賣 _____ 賣東西的 _____ 想一想 _____

都好 _____ 那些 _____ 作買賣的 _____

Ex. 5: In the blanks, write the Chinese equivalents of the following English expressions.

these _____   west _____   all are not going _____

use _____   east _____   time _____

do, make _____   rich _____   business man _____

but _____   those _____   useless _____

things _____   work _____   consider _____

sometimes _____   all are well _____ some people _____

no use to _____   sell things _____   poor _____

trade (simplified) _____   correct (simplified) _____

LESSON IV   43

Ex. 6: The expressions in each group may be preceded by
        the character that heads the group. Place the
        head character before each, and after the new
        expression give the English meaning.

```
        有                  沒                  不
    ___錢_____          ___甚麼____         __去_____

    ___事_____          ___事_____          __對_____

    __時候_____          ___有_____          __用_____

    __些人_____          ___錢_____          __來_____

    ___用_____          ___用_____          __要_____
```

Ex. 7: In the blank space beside each character write a
        character (or characters) which form(s) a combina-
        tion and give the meaning of each combination.

1. ___是_____   6. 好____人_____

2. ___西_____   7. ____了_____

3. 買_____   8. ____想_____

4. ____賣_____   9. ____候_____

5. 有_____   10. ____事_____

Ex. 8: For each set of sentences and phrases, select characters given above the set and write them in the blanks to make good sense.

A. 麼　東　候　對　西　甚　時　不

    1. 他 ___ ___ ___ 來？
    2. 先生說：「___ ___！ ___ ___！」
    3. 他買 ___ ___ ___ ___？
    4. 你那天作 ___ ___？

B. 都　人　些　不　好　去

    1. 那個地方有 ___ ___ ___ 。
    2. 他們 ___ ___ ___ 。
    3. 我們 ___ 好。
    4. 那 ___ 人 ___ ___ 。

C. 作　錢　事　些　想

    1. 他們 ___ ___ 。
    2. 這 ___ 人沒 ___ 。
    3. 你 ___ 不 ___ 先去？
    4. 我不 ___ ___ 買賣。

LESSON IV

Ex. 9: Translate the following into English.

1. 他們甚麼時候來？

2. 有些人不去。

3. 你賣甚麼東西？

4. 我那個時候沒錢。

5. 學生都不去。

6. 作買賣的說：「你們不用去。」

7. 先生對我們很好。

8. 我想說中國話，可是他說：「你不用說中國話。」

9. 他們都很有錢。

10. 那些中國人都來。

Ex. 10: Translate the following into Chinese.

1. What time will you (pl.) come?

2. He is very rich.

3. Neither of them is going.

4. "That's not right. She is Chinese."

5. What things does he sell?

6. It's useless to speak Chinese.

7. There are a good many people in back.

8. That businessman is very good.

9. He is Chinese, but he does not speak Chinese.

10. He said to me, "You may go to Germany."

LESSON IV

Ex. 11: SEEK AND FIND. Find and circle the Chinese equivalent for each of the English items below the box. Put the letter of the English item inside the circle you make. Note that the items are expressions that may include more than one character, and the characters may run horizontally, vertically, diagonally, and either left or right.

時	好	了	可	候	可	說	國
後	可	是	時	十	時	賣	話
來	多	九	先	生	東	買	作
小	外	前	兒	不	人	下	上
很	西	東	好	對	那	些	有
甚	頭	們	你	看	個	錢	沒
麼	對	少	他	事	給	東	要
了	在	也	作	子	我	地	方

a. but, however   b. those   c. things   d. what

e. time   f. work   g. poor   h. that's right

i. incorrect   j. speak   k. give   l. good looking

B. Exercises on the Story

Ex. 12: Complete the sentence by copying the correct characters from the story.

1. ___ ___ ___ ___ ___ ___ ___ syìng Jāng.

2. ___ ___ chéng ___ ___ ___ ___ ___ pù ___,
   ___ ___ ___ ___ ___.

3. "___ ___ yi ___ ___ yi ___ ___ ___ pù ___
   ___ ___ ___ dyǎn ___ ___?"

4. "___ ___ jǎu dyǎn ___ ___ ___."

5. ___ hwèi ___ ___ ___ ___ ?"

6. ___ tīng ___ ___, ___ ___ ___ dzwèi ___ jǐn
   ___ ___, jyòu ___ ___ ___ ___.

7. ___ děi jrdau, ___ ___ ___ ___ ___ ___ ___
   ___ dzwèi ___ ___ ___, ___ dzwèi ___ ___ ___
   ___.

8. 可 ___ ___ ___ ___ ___ ___ ___ yi ___ !

9. Li ___ ___ : "___ ___ ___ ___ ___ syíng ___
   syíng?"

10. "___ syíng ___ ___ ___, ___ ___ ___ ___."

LESSON IV   49

Ex. 13:   Answer the following questions on the story.

1. Jāng 先生是 shéi？他作甚麼事？

2. Lǐ 二是 shéi？他從哪兒來？

3. Lǐ 二對老 Jāng 說甚麼？

4. Lǐ 二不會作甚麼？

5. 老 Jāng 可 yi jyāu Lǐ 二作甚麼？

6. 買東西的人都想作甚麼？

7. Jāng 先生對 Lǐ 二說賣東西的人 děi 對，買東西的人說甚麼？

8. 你想 Lǐ 二可 yi 作買賣嗎？

9. 你 hwèi 賣東西嗎？

10. 你 syǐng 甚麼？

C. Exercises on Character Shape and Origin

Ex. 14: In the blank beside each character write the first and last strokes. One example is given.

可 一 , 亅   些 _____   對 _____   事 _____   錢 _____

想 _____   用 _____   賣 _____   候 _____   時 _____

Ex. 15: In each of the following groups there is a common element. Write that common element.

a　你　候　作　他

b　我　錢　國

c　可　給　國　說　話

d　東　都　時　是

LESSON IV

D. Review Exercises

Ex. 16: Translate the following into Chinese.
(write simplified characters)

1. I am a Chinese.

2. Where is your son going?

3. They gave me four pieces of candy.

4. What time will they go?

5. None of them is German (i.e. All of them are not. . .).

6. Those Chinese are all in business.

7. That rich man doesn't say anything.

8. Where is the teacher?

9. He's in back.

10. Those two men in front are also Chinese.

Ex. 17: Rewrite the following expressions, replacing simplified characters with full characters, and vice versa.

1. 甚麼時候？ _____

2. 卖东西： _____

3. 對了： _____

4. 买卖： _____

5. 没钱： _____

6. 时候不对： _____

THE CHARACTER BOOK

LESSON V

A. Exercises on Character Meaning and Use

Ex. 1: Draw lines connecting the Chinese and English equivalents.

會	ask (regular)
寫	know how to (simplified)
饭	sun, day
日	only
问	invite, request
字	volume
会	write (simplified)
吃	know how to (regular)
写	learn
坐	meal, rice
問	eat
就	ask (simplified)
本	character
學	write (regular)
请	sit

Ex. 2: Give Yale Romanization for the following expressions.

1. 請坐

2. 日本

3. 不能去

4. 學生

5. 回來

6. 寫字

7. 問我

8. 吃飯

9. 請問

10. 就有

11. 會作事

12. 回去

13. 中國字

14. 能買

15. 十本

LESSON V   55

Ex. 3:   Write the letter of the English equivalent in
           the blank space beside each Chinese expression.

           回   _____   a. know how to

           可以   _____   b. please sit down

           能   _____   c. Chinese character

           吃飯   _____   d. may

           日本   _____   e. able

           就有   _____   f. return

           寫字   _____   g. write

           會   _____   h. eat

           請坐   _____   i. Japan

           中國字 _____   j. only have

Ex. 4: In the blanks write the English equivalents for the following Chinese expressions.

不能去 _____ 可以 _____ 寫字 _____ 日本 _____

吃飯 _____ 坐下 _____ 問…好 _____ 中飯 _____

回來 _____ 三個字 _____ 能買 _____ 會說話 _____

学生 _____ 請吃飯 _____ 会做事 _____ 請問 _____

Ex. 5: In the blanks, write the Chinese equivalents for the following English expressions.

please be seated _____   best regards to... _____

know how to _____   only _____   write (characters) _____

return to one's native country _____   Japan _____

able to buy _____   Please may I ask? _____

noon meal _____   sit down _____   may _____

cannot come _____   four words _____   student _____

study Chinese _____   eat (meal) _____   return here _____

study to write Chinese characters _____

invite people to dinner _____   write (simp.) _____

ask (simp.) _____   learn (simp.) _____

LESSON V

Ex. 6: Select from column b characters that make expressions with characters in column a. Write those characters in the blanks and give the meaning of the expressions you make.

a   b

日 ___ _____   囘
___ 字 _____   坐
___ 生 _____   問
就 ___ _____   有
吃 ___ _____   本
___ 坐 _____   寫
___ 好 _____   會
請 ___ _____   請
___ 國 _____   學
___ 說話 _____   飯

Ex. 7: For each set of sentences and phrases, select characters given above the set and write them in the blanks to make good sense.

A. 本　吃　會　日

　1. 他是 ____ ____ 人。
　2. 那六 ____ shū 是我的。
　3. 他想 ____ ____ ____ 飯。
　4. 我不 ____ 說 ____ ____ 話。

B. 字　就　寫　會

　1. 我 ____ ____ 中國 ____ 。
　2. 我們都不 ____ ____ 。
　3. 我們 ____ 有一 dyǎn 兒錢。
　4. 我兒子 ____ ____ 三個 ____ 。

C. 以　學　可

　1. 先生說：「你們 ____ ____ 來。」
　2. 我想 ____ 寫中國字。
　3. 他不想 ____ 寫日本字。
　4. ____ 生不 ____ ____ 吃飯。

D. 問　囘　請

　1. 你不 ____ 國嗎？
　2. ____ 坐！ ____ 坐！
　3. ____ ____ ，學 syàu 在哪兒？

LESSON V   59

Ex. 8:   The blanks in the following sentences may be
         filled in by one or more of the three expressions
         會, 能, 可以 . Fill in the blank correctly
         and translate your sentences.

1. 先生都____說日本話。

2. 你們____買日本 shū。

3. 他們想說中國話，可是不____說。

4. 先生對學生說：「你們_____去。」

5. 他不____賣他的 chē。

6. 我不 ____ 說日本話。我們說中國話好不好？

7. 學生都_____gēn 先生說話。

8. 我兒子不____寫字。

9. 日本人都____寫中國字嗎？

10. 你甚麼時候____來？

Ex. 9: Translate the following sentences into English.

1. 我問他吃飯了沒有。
2. 他很會作事。
3. 會寫日本字的人都會說日本話。
4. 他說他不能去。
5. 那天我不能來。
6. 我就有兩個。
7. Wáng 先生不想吃飯。
8. 請問，你是日本人嗎？
9. 學中國話的人都是好人。
10. 你可以囘國。

LESSON V   61

Ex. 10: Translate the following sentences into Chinese.
        (sentences one to five-simplified, six to ten-regular)

1. He's inviting me to eat.

2. Please sit.

3. He'll ask me.

4. I can't speak Japanese.

5. I can buy (it).

6. I only have one.

7. All the students want to come.

8. He writes Chinese characters daily.

9. We may return home.

10. He's learning to write (characters).

B. Exercises on the Story

Ex. 11: Crossword.

Down

1. You may ask me.
2. will go right after eating
3. Japanese student
4. How about it?
5. Come back first
6. write (characters)

Across

1. You invite him to eat (something).
5. teacher, husband
6. write a letter
7. lunch
8. best regards to
9. only have ten volumes
10. I can not go.
11. Chinese characters
12. come up

LESSON V   63

Ex. 12: Questions on the story.

1. 有一nyán Jāng先生的日本 péngyou 請他作甚麼？

2. Jāng 先生會不會說日本話？

3. Jāng 先生要 gēn shéi 學日本話？

4. 那個 péngyou jyāu 他說日本話了嗎？

5. 他說甚麼不要 jīn ？

6. 日本人是不是都 dǔng 中國字？

7. Jāng 先生想在飯 gwǎn 兒吃哪些東西？

8. "Tang" 字在日本是甚麼 yìsz ？

9. Jāng 先生在飯 gwǎn 兒吃了些甚麼？

10. Jāng 先生回國以後，chángchang gēn 人說甚麼？

Ex. 13: CONTROLLED PARAGRAPH. Rewrite paragraph #1 of the story in Lesson 5. In your rewrite, make 我 the subject who has the friend that goes travelling, and make English the language that everyone there can speak. The country you travel to is France. Eliminate references to third person, e.g. the first sentence. Thus, your first sentence will begin 有一 nyán, 我的一 wèi Dé 國 péngyou ...

LESSON V

C. Review Exercises

Ex. 14: Fill in the blanks, with one character per blank.

1. 他們要 ___ ___ 錢？

2. 先生 ___ ___ 生說：「Byé 問我」

3. 那些日本人 ___ 很 ___ ___ 中國字。

4. 他 ___ ___ ___ 來？

5. 沒 ___ 的人不 ___ ___ ___ 西。

6. 你先生用 ___ ___ 話 gēn ___ 說？

7. ___ 生說 ___ 們 ___ ___ 去。

8. ___ 我看一 ___ ，好嗎？

9. 很 ___ 看的人都是 ___ ___ 嗎？

10. 日 ___ 人 ___ ___ 寫 ___ 字嗎？

Ex. 15: Rewrite the following expressions replacing simplified characters with full characters, and vice versa.

1. 請問：
2. 学生：
3. 吃飯：
4. 会不会：
5. 写字：
6. 中国饭：

THE CHARACTER BOOK: REVIEW LESSON A
(Lessons 1-5)
Exercises

Note: In the four review lessons contained in this workbook, it is intended that students should work through the material as rapidly as possible. These lessons are provided as a <u>quick</u> review of material which you should already know quite well. If you run into difficulty, turn back to the lessons in RCI and in this book right away. Don't let lapses of memory frustrate you. Everyone has them, and the authors of this book probably have more than you will ever have. At the same time, don't let insufficiently mastered material become a block to further progress. Unlike the regular lessons, the review lessons are not organized according to a single pattern. Rather, the material is given in deliberately jumbled order so as to make the review less predictable.

Ex. 1: SEEK AND FIND. Find and circle the Chinese equivalents for each of the English items below the box. Put the letter of the English item inside the circle you make. Note that the items are expressions which may include more than one character, and the characters in any expression may run horizontally, vertically, or diagonally, and either left or right.

REVIEW LESSON A   67

Ex. 1:   SEEK AND FIND.

好	要	沒	給	書	作	事	的	子
人	不	方	西	看	他	說	們	不
都	請	吃	日	生	的	話	我	對
坐	能	回	學	賣	們	少	錢	有
買	會	人	些	好	買	多	九	個
賣	想	時	國	中	坐	作	字	飯
用	候	就	八	外	的	寫	問	吃

a. student   g. Don't!
b. write (words)   h. talk
c. eat (meal)   i. foreigner
d. engage in a trade   j. our, ours
e. time   k. a good many people
f. rich   l. incorrect

Ex. 2: Divide the following characters into five groups. Each group will be identified by a common component. Circle that component in each character.

請　女　說
要　們　個
他　後　作
大　候　回
很　你　吃
問　話

Ex. 3: Transform the following statements into questions.

1. 他會說中國話。

2. 我沒寫字。

3. 你是日本人。

4. 學生們都買外國 shū。

5. 他的話很對。

REVIEW LESSON A   69

Ex. 4:   In the blanks, write the English equivalents of
          the Chinese items.

甚麼 _____ 地方 _____ 去 _____ 多 _____

來 _____   好看 _____ 兒子 _____ 時候 _____

沒用 _____ 可是 _____ 三天 _____ 也 _____

他 _____   給 _____   要 _____   中國話 _____

先生 _____ 很小 _____

Ex. 5:   Translate the following into English.

1. 日本人都會說中國話嗎？

2. 我們的學 syàu 就有一個。

3. 他們很會寫中國字。

4. 我天天都賣很多東西。

5. 前頭是甚麼？

Ex. 6: Answer the following questions in Chinese.

1. 你會說中國話嗎？
2. 那個人是不是外國人？
3. 我的兒子在裏頭嗎？
4. 先生說我們可以寫中國字嗎？
5. 你是不是天天吃中國飯？

Ex. 7: Use each of the following characters to make one expression of more than one character.

1. 對	6. 用	11. 看	16. 沒
2. 請	7. 想	12. 子	17. 上
3. 以	8. 候	13. 好	18. 後
4. 字	9. 事	14. 這	19. 不
5. 本	10. 的	15. 甚	20. 些

REVIEW LESSON A   71

Ex. 8:   Transform the following sentences into negative
         sentences.

1. 他有很多錢。

2. 我們在學 syàu 學中國話。

3. 這些東西是我的。

4. 我想到外國去。

5. 下月他想到這兒來。

Ex. 9:   In the blanks, write the Chinese equivalent of the
         English items.

foreign tongue_____   inside_____   mine_____

very large_____   don't have_____   below_____

also_____   quite a few_____   student_____

son_____   only_____   may_____   able_____

Chinese characters_____   know how to_____

sit down_____   ask_____   please_____

eat (meal)_____

After completion, make a list of any simplified forms that
occur in the above terms.

Ex. 10: Translate the following sentences into Chinese.

1. He's inviting us to eat.

2. The teacher said, 'Please sit down.'

3. I go to school everday, but he doesn't.

4. They are going to Japan to study Japanese.

5. I only have fifty of them.

6. I can speak Chinese.

7. 'He's in business? What does he sell?'

8. The teacher said, 'You are all correct.'

9. He wants to think it over.

10. When will they come?

REVIEW LESSON A   73

Ex. 11: Write the Yale romanization after each character.

國 _____ 去 _____ 子 _____ 時 _____

作 _____ 事 _____ 月 _____ 上 _____

沒 _____ 在 _____ 了 _____ 裏 _____

學 _____ 少 _____ 些 _____ 想 _____

是 _____ 坐 _____ 吃 _____ 十 _____

Ex. 12: Complete the following sentences. Consult the
         English expression in the parentheses.

1. 他會說日本話，可是 _____ (not Chinese)

2. 學生們想吃，可是 _____ (the teacher does not)

3. 我就有一個，可是 _____ (he has three)

4. 你們想去，可是 _____ (I don't)

5. 他們是中國人，可是 _____ (I am not)

Ex. 13: Write the Yale romanization after each combination.

甚麼_____ 沒有_____ 我們_____ 他的_____

兩個_____ 地方_____ 這裏_____ 前頭_____

先生_____ 多少_____ 很好_____ 好看_____

作事_____ 有錢_____ 對了_____ 可是_____

Ex. 14: Translate the following sentences into Chinese.

1. What do you want to say?

2. Do you know how to write Chinese characters?

3. He is unable to work.

4. May we buy those things?

5. There are twelve of them in front.

6. There are 99 Japanese students eating Chinese food.

7. That man is asking you how much you want.

8. There are a good many people wanting to buy these things.

9. He is in business (trade).

10. He has business to do.

REVIEW LESSON A

Ex. 15: CROSS CHARACTER PUZZLE. Complete the following just like a crossword puzzle.

Down

1. None of their words are correct.
2. yours
3. useful
4. no money
5. many affairs
6. Chinese language
7. go to the front
8. do business
9. the small one

Across

1. What does he give you?
3. sometimes
4. useless
6. lunch
8. to work
10. how much money?
11. to talk
12. do not plan (want) to buy
13. back
14. the place where things are sold

Ex. 16: Rewrite the following sentences, replacing simplified characters with full characters and vice versa.

1. 請問,這個中國字是甚麼意思?
2. 我們在這兒賣東西。
3. 那個學生給他寫信嗎?
4. 你会不会说中国话?
5. 他们两个在后头吗?
6. 请问,我们什么时候走?

THE CHARACTER BOOK

LESSON VI

A. Exercises on Character Meaning and Use

Ex. 1: Draw lines connecting the Chinese and English equivalents.

半	leave
听	now
早	friend
還	still (simplified)
叫	half
几	hundred
聽	still (regular)
幾	old
現在	several (simplified)
老	call
百	listen (simplified)
为	early
走	for
朋友	several (regular)
还	listen (regular)

Ex. 2: Write the letter of the English expression in the blank beside the Chinese expression.

___ 爲甚麽   a. friend
___ 一點兒   b. a little bit
___ 幾天   c. hear it said
___ 老了   d. now
___ 還有   e. several days
___ 聽說   f. has aged
___ 八百本   g. still have
___ 現在   h. meaning
___ 意 sz?   i. why?
___ 朋友   j. 800 volumes

LESSON VI   79

Ex. 3:   In the blanks, write the English equivalents of the
          Chinese expressions.

早飯 _____   還要去 _____   好聽 _____

六百個人 _____   叫甚麼 _____   都走了 _____

朋友 _____   幾個人 _____   半天 _____   早上 _____

一點兒 _____   現在 _____   還有 _____   沒意sz _____

Ex. 4:   In the blanks write the Chinese equivalents for
          the English expressions.

take a walk _____   hear it said _____   now _____

700 people _____   morning _____   has aged _____   half _____

friend _____   interesting _____   how many people _____

early _____   a little bit _____   what is (it) called? _____

why _____   still have some _____   quite a few _____

meaning _____   several (simplified) _____

listen (simplified) _____   still (simplified) _____

Ex. 5: Select from column B characters that make expressions with characters in column A. Write those characters in the blanks, and give the meanings of the expressions you have made.

A. 半___ _____ B. 點
   好___個 _____   還
   朋___ _____   聽
   ___了 _____   現
   ___有 _____   百
   好___ _____   幾
   ___甚麼？ _____   老
   ___在 _____   天
   七___個人 _____   友
   ___個人 _____   叫
   一___兒 _____

LESSON VI
                                                                 81

Ex. 6: Complete the sentences below by correctly filling
        in the blanks with expressions from lesson 6 or
        earlier lessons where necessary.

1. 那個東西 ___ ___ 麼？

2. 他 ___ ___ ___ 了。

3. 學生 ___ ___ 不來？

4. 我就有一個 ___ ___ 。

5. 他們 ___ 上不 ___ 飯。

6. 我聽 ___ 你要給我 ___ ___ kwài 錢。

7. 你 ___ ___ 時候回國？我 míng 天 ___ 。

8. 他這 ___ shū 沒意 sz。

9. 我們 ___ syàu 有兩 ___ 個 ___ 生。

10. 我 ___ ___ 七點 jūng ___ 。

11. 他有好 ___ ___ 日本 ___ ___ 。

12. 他 ___ 我去，可 ___ 我不 ___ 。

13. 你那個中國 ___ ___ 甚麼不去？

14. 那個 ___ 人說的話 ___ ___ sz。

15. 我的日本 ___ ___ 很 ___ ___ sz。

Ex. 7: Translate the following sentences into English.

1. 他有很多中國朋友。
2. 他現在在中國。
3. 那個老 tàitai 很有錢。
4. 我 jīn 天沒吃早飯。
5. 你爲甚麼想學中國話？
6. Wáng 先生說的 gù 事都好聽。
7. 這個學 syàu 有一百個學生學中國話。
8. 那個老 tàitai 是我的老朋友。
9. 請你給我一點兒錢。
10. 他叫我走。

LESSON VI   83

Ex. 8:   Translate the following sentences into Chinese.

1. Now I can speak Chinese.

2. Those old men all left.

3. My Japanese friend has 867 Chinese books.

4. What is that thing called?

5. The Chinese that you speak is very good to listen to.

6. Why won't you eat breakfast?

7. He said that writing Chinese characters is very interesting.

8. They want to go again.

9. How many people bought books?

10. Why didn't you eat breakfast?

After completion, make a list of any characters in the sentences above that have simplified equivalents.

Ex. 9:   Crossword Puzzle.

Down

2. he still has
3. one hundred Japanese people
4. you are old now!
5. do not know how
7. all have departed

Across

1. call him
3. a little
4. How many friends do you have?
6. Old people know how to do everything.
8. good to listen to

LESSON VI

B. Exercises on the Story

Ex. 10: Complete the following sentences by referring to the story.

1. 人都____ 他 ____Jàu.

2. 有一天____ ____, ____ Jàu ____ jyē ____ jàn ____ ____ jāng jwō ____ ____.

3. 我也 jīdau, ____ ____ ____ ____ ____ ____ ____ ____ syǐhwan ____ ____ chàng.

4. ____ ____我要 chàng ____ ____ dzwèi ____ ____ gē ____.

5. 他____ 說了____ ____ byé ____ ____.

6. 說了____ ____。他說話 ____ ____ ____, ____, ____ ____ jēn ____ ____, ____ ____ ____ ____ ____.

7. Chàng 了____ ____ ____, ____ ____ ____ ____.

8. 就有____ ____ ____ ____.

9. 他們都____ dǔng, swǒ ____ ____ ____ ____.

10. 那個人說："____ chàng ____ gē ____ ____ ____ ____ dǔng. ____ ____ ____, yīn ____ ____ jāng jwō ____ ____ ____ ____.

Ex. 11: Answer the following questions on the story.

1. 有一個人 sying Jàu ，人都叫他甚麼？
2. 老 Jàu ài dzwò 甚麼？
3. 他 chàng gē 兒的時候，ywàn 意有甚麼？
4. 有一天甚麼時候老 Jàu 在 jyē shàng ？
5. 他 jàn 在哪兒？
6. 老 Jàu jàn 在 jwō 子上說甚麼？
7. 聽他說話的人多不多？
8. 老 Jàu chàng 了一會兒，人都去哪兒了？
9. 誰還在 jyē 上聽老 Jàu chàng gē 兒？
10. 那個人爲甚麼聽老 Jàu chàng gē 兒？

LESSON VI

Ex. 12:   CONTROLLED COMPOSITION. Copy paragraphs 1 and 2
          of the story. In your version, change Jaù to
          Wáng, and instead of having Mr. Wáng sing, have
          him speak Chinese. So the second sentence will
          read:
          老王 ài 說中國話

C. Exercises on Character Shape and Origin

Ex. 13: Order each group of characters according to the number of strokes in each character.

    a   意 幾 半 現 爲

    b   早 聽 友 百 叫

    c   朋 點 走 老 還

Ex. 14: Identify the common part in each of the following groups and write that part in the blank to the right of the group.

    a   字   子   學   _____

    b   坐   地   在   _____

    c   請   這   話   說   _____

    d   這   還   _____

LESSON VI

D. Review Exercises

Ex. 15: Give the Chinese equivalent for the English expressions in the blanks beside them.

eat (meal)_____ please be seated_____ able to_____

Japan_____ may_____ use_____ that's right_____

business, trade_____ things_____ time_____ go_____

come_____ good looking _____ speak (language)_____

China_____ give_____ few_____ very many_____ these_____

where_____ two Chinese people_____ 954_____

Ex. 16: Answer the following questions in Chinese

1. 你是不是中國人？

2. 你的朋友在哪兒？

3. Wáng 先生為甚麼想走？

4. 他幾點 jūng 吃早飯？

5. Shéi 請你們吃飯？

6. Jàu 先生他們買甚麼東西？

7. 日本人說甚麼話？

8. 他還有那些東西嗎？

9. 他們甚麼時候來？

10. 你很有錢，對不對？

Ex. 17: Rewrite the following sentences, replacing simplified characters with full characters, and vice versa.

1. 你为什么还不走？
2. 現在請你聽我說．
3. 他有几个中国朋友？
4. 我還有一點兒錢．
5. 我听说你会写中国字．

THE CHARACTER BOOK
LESSON VII

A. Exercises on Character Meaning and Use

Ex. 1: Draw lines connecting the Chinese and English equivalents.

兩塊 táng   mother
家   father (regular)
母親   father (simplified)
書   book (simplified)
一塊兒   therefore
今天   today
姓   together (simplified)
父亲   evening
住   yesterday
所以   surname
晚上   tomorrow
第一   book (regular)
一块儿   stay
父親   first
昨天   together (regular)
明天   home, family
书   two pieces of candy

Ex. 2: Write the letter of the English equivalent in the blank beside each Chinese expression.

___ 念書   ___ 父親   a. study
                                   b. yesterday
___ 晚飯   ___ 家裏   c. together
                                   d. father
___ 回家   ___ 所以   e. parents
                                   f. therefore
___ 父母   ___ 中國書   g. return home
                                   h. dinner
___ 一塊兒   ___ 昨天   i. inside the home
                                   j. Chinese books

Ex. 3: In the blanks write the English equivalents for the Chinese expressions.

第一 _____ 所以 _____ 念書 _____ 明天 _____

住在哪兒？_____ 昨天 _____ 母親 _____

不在家 _____ 四塊錢 _____ 回家 _____

買書 _____ 回國 _____ 父母 _____ 晚上 _____

在學 syáu 住 _____ 中國書 _____ 可以 _____

LESSON VII   93

Ex. 4:   In the blanks write the Chinese equivalents for
         the English expressions.

sell books_____   where (does he) live?_____

therefore_____   supper _____   surname_____

yesterday_____   parents_____   in one's house_____

together_____   mother (simplified)_____   study_____

the third book_____   tomorrow_____   father_____

four dollars (simp.) _____   Chinese books (simp.)_____

Ex. 5:   Complete the following sentences.

1. 我母親昨天 _____

2. 那兩塊 táng _____

3. 他不要來，可是 _____

4. 我是中國人，所以 _____

5. 明天晚上 _____

6. 姓 Wáng 的那個人 _____

7. 第四天我們念了 _____

8. 我家有 _____

9. Wáng 先生住在 _____

10. 賣書的 _____

Ex. 6:   Each of the following characters may be used with 天 to make an expression of time. Write out each expression and give the meaning of each.

明　這　天　那　今　昨　半　幾

Ex. 7:   Translate the following time expressions into Chinese.

yesterday   last evening
today   tomorrow morning
daily   half a day
tomorrow   tomorrow evening
this evening   the first day

Ex. 8:   Translate the following into Chinese.

1. that person who lives in the school

2. that old gentleman who is studying

3. those people who came last night

4. that person who went to eat

5. that man sitting there

LESSON VII

Ex. 9: Translate the following sentences into English.

1. 昨天來的學生今天走了。
2. 我還要買一點兒 táng。
3. 那些老人都走了。
4. 那些會中國話的人為甚麼不說中國話？
5. 那個學生不是昨天晚上在你家念書的那個嗎？
6. 姓 Wáng 的那個人明天早上來吃早飯。
7. 我父親昨天沒錢，所以他沒買 táng。
8. 他父母要他作買賣，所以他不能念書。
9. 這是他寫的第一本書。
10. 那塊 táng 是住在我們家那個老人的。

Ex. 10: Translate the following sentences into Chinese.

1. He came on the fifth day.
2. That old man who is surnamed Wang lives at our house.
3. That person who sells books is Japanese.
4. Tomorrow I want to study at home.
5. Last night my parents were not at home, therefore I didn't eat dinner.
6. Today I'm reading Chinese books at school.
7. Those two pieces of candy aren't good to eat.
8. Those two pieces of candy which aren't good to eat are Mr. Wang's.
9. The Chinese that he speaks is very good (to listen to).
10. Why don't your parents leave on the fourth day?

Ex. 11: Translate the following into Chinese.

1. left yesterday
2. came last night
3. eat breakfast this morning
4. didn't return home yesterday
5. didn't study yesterday morning
6. will buy books tomorrow
7. will learn to write Chinese characters next month
8. won't sell books tomorrow
9. didn't write characters yesterday
10. didn't ask me

LESSON VII

Ex. 12: SEEK AND FIND. Find, circle and copy out the Chinese equivalents for the English expressions given at the bottom of the page. Note: the characters in the expressions may be arranged vertically, horizontally, diagonally, left-to-right, or right-to-left.

我	去	候	來	先	晚	早	爲	了
第	前	頭	子	現	飯	下	寫	到
後	東	要	在	友	事	是	字	上
頭	飯	對	字	作	買	賣	還	裏
晚	國	早	學	很	不	中	父	聽
外	中	晚	吃	生	國	也	錢	說
他	書	所	好	書	小	個	塊	用
們	以	可	看	念	兩	死	半	些
問	幾	個	朋	友	九	請	國	都
百	走	有	給	點	七	能	母	東
上	人	沒	多	住	在	哪	兒	西
晚	太	住	少	意	八	坐	塊	叫
的	大	想	錢	沒	以	會	就	姓

1. eat breakfast
2. where does (he) live?
3. Chinese books
4. evening
5. now
6. hear it said
7. several friends
8. half a dollar
9. write characters
10. therefore
11. engage in business, trade
12. things
13. behind
14. foreign country
15. poor
16. study

B. Exercises on the Story

Ex. 13: Answer the following questions on the story.

1. Gù 事裏的 nánhái 子姓甚麼？

2. 他 syǐhwan 不 syǐhwan 念書？

3. 他父母有幾個 hái 子？

4. 他家裏沒錢，對不對？

5. 他們住在哪兒？

6. Jāng 先生天天去甚麼地方？作甚麼？

7. 那個姓 Jāng 的 hái 子天天叫他父親作甚麼？

8. 有一天 Jāng 先生買了甚麼？

9. 那個賣東西的人問甚麼？

10. Jāng 先生說甚麼？

LESSON VII

Ex. 14: The following paragraph is an English translation of paragraph three of the story. Without looking at the book, translate it back into Chinese. Then check your version against the original and recopy yours with corrections.

They lived in the countryside. His father went to the city everyday to work. Everyday, he asked his father to buy a little something for him in the city. In the evening he spoke to his father, (and) his father the next day (would) then buy something for him to bring back. Today he (would) want this, tomorrow he (would) want that. The things he wanted were extremely numerous.

Ex. 15: Controlled composition. Write a short paragraph about a little boy surnamed Wang. He is the only child in his family. His parents are poor. They live in the city. Everyday, his father goes to the countryside to work. The father often buys things to bring back for the son, but the son is a good boy and tells the father not to use his money buying things for him.

C. Exercises on Character Shape and Origin

Ex. 16: The characters in each group share a common component. Circle that component in each character, and write the component in the blank at the right.

a 明 昨 日 晚 東 時 _____

b 明 朋 月 有 _____

c 想 東 本 來 _____

d 親 現 看 _____

e 家 字 寫 _____

f 今 念 住 坐 會 候 作 錢 _____

Ex. 17: Identify the first stroke of each of the following characters. Circle that stroke and write it in the blank to the right of each character.

1. 第 _____   6. 月 _____

2. 所 _____   7. 老 _____

3. 書 _____   8. 聽 _____

4. 母 _____   9. 幾 _____

5. 父 _____   10. 半 _____

LESSON VII

D. Review Exercises

Ex. 18: Translate into Chinese (simplified characters)

1. That boy who doesn't want to study is surnamed Jang.

2. None of the students who live in school are Chinese.

3. Because he is too old, he therefore doesn't work anymore.

4. The very first day I was in China I spoke Chinese.

5. Today my mother is coming for dinner.

6. The teacher said to the students: 'Please be seated.'

7. They asked us: 'Do you know how to write Chinese characters?'

8. Tomorrow I won't be able to go to school.

9. The book seller asked, 'How many books do you want to buy?'

10. That very pretty student speaks excellent Chinese.

Ex. 19: Give the Chinese for the following English expressions.

where?_____ outside_____ behind_____ son_____

last night_____ already arrived_____ may_____

didn't come_____ also, too_____ isn't it so?_____

therefore_____ how many people?_____

half a dollar_____ hear it said_____

Ex. 20: Rewrite the following sentences, replacing simplified characters with full characters and vice versa.

1. 他父亲买了两本书．
2. 這本書幾塊錢？
3. 你们两个人什么时候来？
4. 他母親還會說中國話嗎？
5. 里头的那本书给你母亲．

THE CHARACTER BOOK
LESSON VIII

A. Exercises on Character Meaning and Use

Ex. 1: Draw lines connecting the Chinese and English equivalents.

起來	back door
門外頭	from (regular)
很快	next year
再	very fast
等	again (completed action)
坐着	sitting
慢吃	come out
大門	main gate
又	wait
从	from (simplified)
大鐘	eat slowly
年年	again (prospective action)
知道	know
大钟	big clock (simplified)
從	big clock (regular)
出來	every year
後門	outside the door
明年	get up

Ex. 2: Write the letter of the English equivalent in the blank space beside each Chinese character.

快 ____　　又 ____
再 ____　　門 ____
把 ____　　年 ____
出 ____　　鐘 ____
從 ____　　慢 ____

a. slow
b. from
c. again (completed)
d. fast
e. object marker
f. out
g. again (prospective)
h. door
i. year
j. clock

Ex. 3: Write the number of the Chinese equivalent beside each English expression.

go abroad ____　　a. 快走

wait awhile ____　　b. 起來

slow ____　　c. 有一年

main door ____　　d. 大門

a certain year ____　　e. 等一會兒

know ____　　f. 又

get up ____　　g. 出國

come from his house ____　　h. 慢

again ____　　i. 知道

go quickly ____　　j. 從他家來

LESSON VIII   105

Ex. 4:   In the blanks write the English equivalents for
         the following Chinese expressions.

出去 _____ 等我 _____ 很慢 _____ 知道 _____

三點鐘 _____ 門 _____ 年年 _____ 把 _____

出門 _____   起來 _____   慢吃 _____

又 ____ 等一會兒 ____ 再 _____ 前門 _____

Ex. 5:   Write the Chinese equivalents for the following
         English expressions.

again (completed)_____ from_____ exit_____ door_____

clock_____ year_____ again (prospective)_____ wait_____

fast_____ go quickly_____ eat slowly_____ get up_____

from here to there_____ back door_____

sitting_____ know_____ please come again_____

front door (simp.) _____ big clock (simp.)_____

from (simp.)_____ slow_____ rise_____

Ex. 6:   Translate the following into Chinese.

1. come from his house
2. go to China
3. come from Japan
4. go to his house
5. come out from the school
6. go out from inside the house
7. go to the main gate
8. come to back of the school
9. go out from the front door
10. come to Japan

Ex. 7:   Translate the following into Chinese.

1. please come again
2. came again
3. left again
4. go to China again
5. went to Japan again

LESSON VIII

Ex. 8: Translate the following into English.

1. 我們在門外頭等他。
2. 我不能再給他錢了。
3. 我去年出國的時候從中國到日本走了二十天。
4. 我們走的時候，他說：「請他來。」
5. 他們從後門出去。
6. Wáng 先生不知道那個大鐘是 shéi 的。
7. 他走的很快，我走的很慢。
8. 我今天等你來。
9. 你幾點鐘起來？
10. Wáng 先生明年從哪兒來？

Ex. 9 : Translate the following into Chinese.

1. This clock is very fast. That clock is very slow.

2. Do you know who he is?

3. Please, may I ask, where is the main door?

4. Why don't you come from there to here?

5. He told me to come out quickly.

6. Every year they take a boat from China to here.

7. What time do you get up?

8. He ordered me to wait awhile.

9. I know where that large clock is.

10. I know why he's not coming.

After completion, make a list of any simplified equivalents that occur in the above sentences.

LESSON VIII

Ex. 10: SEEK AND FIND. Locate, circle, and write out the Chinese equivalents for the English items given below.

子	去	紙	第	去	國	書
義	走	門	一	來	去	上
來	等	來	個	出	起	下
我	一	大	再	又	來	到
字	會	問	很	請	甚	從
了	兒	快	好	作	這	這
來	慢	來	高	兒	門	去
又	到	快	到	子	後	出
年	道	那	走	今	前	家
念	兒	個	筆	天	年	鐘
他	怕	人	把	道	後	點
車	家	我	知	慢	叫	七
人	裏	不	到	吃	着	人
九	前	去	了	飯	坐	大
個	頭	了	快	中	打	人

1. very fast
2. from here to there
3. eat slowly
4. come out
5. sitting
6. don't know
7. 7:00
8. this year
9. back door
10. please come again
11. came again
12. go quickly
13. wait for a while
14. get up
15. go out

B. Exercises on the Story

Ex. 11: Answer the following questions on the story.

1. 有一年我作甚麼了？

2. 我為甚麼請幾位朋友 bāng 我 máng？

3. 我有一個朋友有甚麼？

4. 有一個東西我沒叫他們 bān，那是甚麼？

5. Byé 的東西是 shéi bān 的？

6. 那個鐘大不大？

7. 我把那個鐘從哪兒 bān 到了哪兒？

8. 為甚麼我在 jyē 上走的慢？

9. 有一個人看着我作甚麼？

10. 那個人問我甚麼？

Ex. 12: CONTROLLED COMPOSITION. Rewrite paragraphs two and three, making the following change. You are moving a very large table 很大的棹子 The onlooker on the street asks you why you don't eat dinner at home.

LESSON VIII   111

Ex. 13:   CONTROLLED COMPOSITION. Write one paragraph
          about moving with several friends helping you
          move. Because you are a student, most of what
          you have to move is books. Because none of your
          friends has a car, you must move the books by
          hand very slowly over a long distance.

       C.   Exercises on Character Shape and Origin

Ex. 14:   Circle the first stroke of each of the following
          characters, and write that stroke in the space to
          the right.

1. 知 _____   6. 又 _____

2. 道 _____   7. 門 _____

3. 慢 _____   8. 着 _____

4. 起 _____   9. 鐘 _____

5. 出 _____   10. 年 _____

Ex. 15:   Circle the common component of each character in
          each group, and write that component in the
          blank to the right.

     a   起 走   _____

     b   們 門 問   _____

     c   知 請 說 話   _____

D. Review Exercises

Ex. 16. Translate the following sentences into Chinese.

1. I want to study Chinese tomorrow.

2. He moved the big clock to outside the door.

3. I get up everyday at 7:00 am.

4. The teacher said to the students, 'Go quickly! Go quickly!'

5. They eat on the local train.

6. He came from China to France.

7. I know that he picked up the pen and went out.

8. The first day that I was in school, a student named Wang came to study with me.

9. Last night my mother returned home at 12:00.

10. I hear that you have many foreign friends.

11. That old person is still here; why didn't he leave earlier?

12. The rice that you bought wasn't good.

13. Where are those things that you gave me?

14. Wait a while. I'll go home with you.

15. How many hours are needed to go from your house to school?

16. Please take that large table and move it upstairs.

17. Last year he bought a big clock.

18. Where did you live when you studied Chinese in China?

Ex. 17: Rewrite the following sentences, replacing simplified characters with full characters and vice versa.

1. 大钟在这个门后头。
2. 你甚麼時候從中國回來?
3. 他父亲从什么地方来?
4. 這個鐘幾塊錢?
5. 我们在门里头等他一会儿。

THE CHARACTER BOOK
LESSON IX

A. Exercises on Character Meaning and Use

Ex. 1: Draw lines connecting the English and Chinese equivalents.

件	polite measure (for persons)
意思	don't
別	expensive (simplified)
进	send, deliver
太	too
愛	take, carry
貴	love (simplified)
星期	thing, affair
因爲	expensive (regular)
行	enter (simplified)
送	week
爱	enter (regular)
位	because
事情	be satisfactory, "can do"
進	meaning
贵	love (regular)
拿	measure for article

114

LESSON IX

Ex. 2: Write the letter of the English meaning beside the Chinese equivalent.

不太貴	_____	a. not too expensive
三個星期	_____	b. see a friend off
行不行	_____	c. too much
別的	_____	d. because
拿走	_____	e. Sunday
太多	_____	f. meaning
因為	_____	g. two things
星期天	_____	h. don't leave
意思	_____	i. other
進去	_____	j. Mrs., wife
送朋友	_____	k. pick up
別走	_____	l. come in
愛念書	_____	m. Your surname?
送給你	_____	n. take away
太太	_____	o. won't do
拿起來	_____	p. give (it) to you
進來	_____	q. love to study
貴姓	_____	r. go in
不行	_____	s. ok or not?
兩件事情	_____	t. 3 weeks
星期三	_____	u. Wednesday

Ex. 3: Write the English equivalents beside the Chinese expressions.

事情 _____   有意思 _____   別人 _____

這位先生 _____   行不行 _____   拿起來 _____

進去 _____   我愛念書 _____   兩件事情 _____

別的 _____   沒有意思 _____   四個星期 _____

進來 _____   星期四 _____   貴姓 _____

因為 _____   別去 _____   那件事情 _____

Ex. 4: Write the Chinese equivalents beside the English expressions.

this affair _____   don't leave _____   dull _____

ok or not? _____   deliver _____   too much _____   week _____

because _____   enter _____   take things _____   others _____

too expensive _____   take away _____   this lady _____

2 matters of business _____   your surname? _____

love to study (simp.) _____   come in (simp.) _____

expensive (simp.) _____

Identify and list any simplified equivalents that appear among the terms in Exercises 3 and 4.

LESSON IX

Ex. 5: Fill in the blanks with characters from Lesson Nine or earlier lessons (when necessary).

1. 這個 ___ ___ ___ 我想吃中國飯。
2. 先生說：「___ 叫他 ___ ___。這兒的學生 ___ 多了。
3. 那 ___ 老 ___ ___ 說：「我有兩 ___ 事 ___ 要　　你說。」
4. 這 ___ 學生說我寫的書 ___ ___ ___ ！
5. 我們明天走，___ ___ ___ ？
6. 請你把那些東西都 ___ ___ 。
7. 我 ___ 念書，可是先生叫我們 ___ 念書。
8. 我日本朋友 ___ ___ 我一本很 ___ 的書。
9. ___ 為他沒錢，所以他沒來。
10. 我 ___ ___ 把我的書都 ___ ___ 了。

Ex. 6:   Translate the following into Chinese.

1. Give him a little money.

2. Give her a book.

3. Give them something.

4. Give the students an expensive book.

5. Give the old lady a big clock.

Ex. 7:   Translate the following into Chinese.

1. ok or not?

2. good or not?

3. big or not?

4. small or not?

5. slow or not?

Ex. 8:   Translate the following into Chinese.

1. too much?

2. very expensive?

3. very many?

4. too few?

5. too slow?

LESSON IX

Ex. 9: Transform the following clauses into descriptive clauses. One example is given.

Example: 送給他錢 ⟶ 送給他的錢

1. 送給我朋友一本書
2. 愛他朋友
3. 東西都拿走了
4. 那本書太貴
5. 那個人等我

Ex. 10: Translate the following into Chinese.

1. Take this thing out.

2. Bring that thing in.

3. Give this thing to him.

4. Tell my friend to get up.

5. Take that thing away.

Ex. 11: Translate the following into Chinese.

1. The clock that I gave him is not too expensive.

2. He likes to talk too much.

3. Please take those things away on Sunday.

4. This matter is very interesting.

5. I'll go together with that old lady, ok?

6. I did not know that he had come in.

7. He said to his wife, "I love you!"

8. Because he didn't have any money, he couldn't buy those expensive books.

9. Those four gentlemen all came from China today.

10. I'll give it to him on Sunday, OK?

Identify and list any simplified equivalents that occur in the above sentences.

LESSON IX   121

Ex. 12:   Write a sentence or two in Chinese that will
          be appropriate to the situation give below.
          Do not translate the sentences.

1. He doesn't have enough money.

2. On Sunday I need to study at home.

3. Those things are all over the floor.

4. They've been outside for 3 hours.

5. The books are $20.00 each.

6. He has no interest in that book.

7. The teacher didn't want the students to talk.

8. He asked his mother why it wasn't all right.

9. The old lady couldn't go home by herself.

10. What she said to the man she was very fond of.

B. Exercises on the Story

Ex. 13: Answer the following questions.

1. 那個學生姓甚麼？
2. 姓 Jāng 的那位先生愛作甚麼？
3. 姓 Lǐ 的那位先生愛請人到家裏作甚麼？
4. 那個學生為甚麼不能念書？
5. 有一天那個學生把 shéi 請到他家裏去了？
6. 學生 gēn Jāng 先生，Lǐ 先生說甚麼？
7. Jāng 先生為甚麼說 bān 家很不 róngyi？
8. 那個學生想送他們幾塊錢？
9. 第二天兩位先生對那個學生說甚麼？
10. 他們兩位 bān 到哪兒去了？

LESSON IX

Ex. 14: The following sentences are similar to ones in the story. They are incomplete. Complete them, and copy the full new sentence out. In your completion, use the expression(s) in parentheses.

1. 我有一個朋友姓 Wáng ，他住　　　（別人）

2. 那個 fáng 子很小，可是　　　（太）

3. 他後頭 wū 子裏住着　　　（位）

4. 因為他很　syihwan hē jyǒu　　　（星期六）

5. 那個作買賣的有一點兒 (any way you want)

6. 外頭有一位老先生，小 Wáng 請　　　（進）

7. Wáng 太太說　　　（事情，件）

8. Wáng 先生說他　　　（愛，沒有意思）

9. Wáng 先生天天賣很多東西　　　（因，貴）

10. 明天我不能來　　　（因，送）

Ex. 15:   CONTROLLED COMPOSITION. Write a composition based on the following information. Your composition should be short, and it should <u>not</u> simply be a translation of the summary below.

You are a student. On Sunday you went out to buy books. You have no money, and the books are too expensive. But one bookseller sees that you love to study and says he'll tell you something very good. He says if you will move all the books from his store to the school, he'll give you five books. After you have moved 900 books, he gives you five books that you do not want.

C.   Exercise on Character Shape and Origin

Ex. 16:   Circle the common component in the characters of each group and write that component in the blank to the right.

a   送   這   進   道   _____

b   太   天   大   因   _____

c   情   快   慢   _____

d   愛   念   思   意   想   _____

e   貴   買   賣   _____

LESSON IX   125

D. Review Exercises

Ex. 17: CONTROLLED COMPOSITION. Write the following
        composition, but do not translate it.

One day you went shopping for Chinese books. It was
Sunday, and the stores that were open were few. The first
store you went to had books that were too expensive. The
second store had less expensive books, but you didn't understand them. The third store had books that were both cheap
and comprehensible. They were all in English.

Ex. 18: Cross Character Puzzle. Complete the following just as you would a crossword puzzle.

Down

1. because it's not interesting
2. two matters
3. how many people (polite)
4. not too expensive
5. give (it) to you (as a gift)
6. week

Across

2. two old ladies
4. won't do
7. (Your) honorable surname?
8. have nothing to do (have no affairs)
9. I love you.

THE CHARACTER BOOK
LESSON X

A. Exercises on Character Meaning and Use

Ex. 1: Draw lines connecting the English and Chinese.

紙	ten thousand (simplified)
眞	true
誰	who (simplified)
房子	writing instruments (simplified)
千	hand
笔	room
女	new
男	ten thousand (regular)
万	watch
屋子	letter
常	writing instrument (regular)
纸	who (regular)
新	female
手表	male
手	house
谁	paper (simplified)
信	often
筆	paper (regular)
萬	one thousand

THE CHARACTER BOOK

Ex. 2: Put the letter of the English equivalent in the space beside the character.

___ 男   ___ 眞   a. letter
___ 女   ___ 新   b. male
___ 常   ___ 誰   c. 1,000
___ 千   ___ 筆   d. paper
___ 萬   ___ 紙   e. room
___ 房   ___ 信   f. watch
___ 表   ___ 屋   g. often
___ 手   h. female
                             i. hand
                             j. true
                             k. new
                             l. writing instrument
                             m. house
                             n. 10,000
                             o. who

Ex. 3: Write the English equivalents in the blanks beside the Chinese.

男人 _____ 女兒 _____ 眞好 _____

五千人 _____ 書房 _____ 手表 _____

寫信 _____ 外國筆 _____ 常常 _____

女朋友 _____ 新的 _____ 屋子 _____

誰來了 _____ 常來 _____ chú 房 _____

信紙 _____ 男學生 _____

LESSON X

Ex. 4: Write the Chinese equivalents in the blanks beside the English.

letter paper_____ new pen_____ not often_____ who_____

truly_____ men students_____ house_____ 1,000_____

10,000_____ daughter_____ study (n.)_____ watch_____

400,000,000_____ write a letter_____

man_____ room_____ 3,000 people_____ very new_____

frequently_____ really good_____ paper_____

foreign pen (simp.)_____ who came? (simp.)_____

20,000 (simp.)_____

Ex. 5: Answer these questions, keeping 誰 as the subject in your answers. Translate your answers. One example is given.

1. 誰不來？ Ans.: 誰都不來 No one is coming.

2. 誰不愛念書？

3. 誰沒有錢？

4. 誰不會說中國話？

5. 昨天晚上誰沒寫中國字？

Ex. 6:   Combine each of the expressions in column A with as many of those in column B as are possible. Translate the combinations you make.

A		B	
裏		房子	
外頭		屋子	
上		信	
上頭		門	
前頭		鐘	

Ex. 7:   Listed below are activities which you already know how to write about in Chinese. Make up a sentence telling about someone doing each of the activities, and include in your sentences the <u>location</u> of the activity. <u>Don't use the same location in more than one sentence.</u>

1. eat dinner

2. study

3. read Japanese books

4. write Chinese

5. eat breakfast

6. write with a Chinese pen

7. sell stationery

8. buy books

9. listen to the teacher speak a foreign language

10. ask Mr. Wang how to get to the university

LESSON X

Ex. 8: Translate the Chinese numbers into Arabic numbers and the Arabic numbers into Chinese. Work as fast as you can.

1. 一萬 _____
2. 兩萬 _____
3. 十萬 _____
4. 六百萬 _____
5. 七千萬 _____
6. 五萬萬 _____
7. 九百三十六 _____
8. 八千九百萬 _____
9. 四千八百三十九 _____
10. 三十六萬七千八百四十五

11. 10,000 _____
12. 9,999 _____
13. 1,523 _____
14. 685 _____
15. 100,000,000 _____
16. 45,000,000 _____
17. 756,243 _____
18. 25,000 _____
19. 58,000,000 _____
20. 9,253 _____

Ex. 9:   Translate into Chinese.

1. 100 books

2. one million people

3. two hundred and fifty-three million dollars

4. 353 Japanese books

5. 6 girl friends

6. 85 foreign friends

7. one mother and one father

8. 37,500 students

9. 8 million merchants

10. 2 million Chinese books

LESSON X

Ex. 10: Complete the following sentences.

1. Wáng 先生叫我多念書，可是＿＿＿＿＿＿＿＿
2. 屋子裏的那個女學生＿＿＿＿＿＿＿＿＿＿
3. 房子後頭的那個新來的學生＿＿＿＿＿＿
4. 誰＿＿＿＿＿＿＿＿＿＿＿＿＿？
5. 誰＿＿＿＿＿＿＿＿＿＿＿＿．
6. 那本書眞有＿＿＿＿＿＿＿＿＿
7. 他給他母親寫了＿＿＿＿＿＿＿＿
8. 因爲信紙很貴，所以＿＿＿＿＿＿＿
9. 他的新手表眞好看，＿＿＿＿＿＿＿
10. 我大女兒＿＿＿＿＿＿＿＿＿＿＿

Ex. 11: Translate the following sentences into Chinese.

1. These few weeks he hasn't written to his parents.

2. China has 900 million people.

3. When Mr. Wang came, he was in the study reading a book.

4. That house is really large and good looking: $50,000 isn't too expensive.

5. No one wants to use the new money.

6. Where does your new wrist watch come from?

7. The stationery that she uses to write her boyfriend is really expensive.

8. His daughter comes often.

9. Males and females both want that new house.

10. He often writes to his teacher.

LESSON X

B. Exercises on the Story

Ex. 12: Answer the following questions on the story.

1. 買東西爲甚麼不一 dìng 好？
2. 男人買東西的時候常常想甚麼？
3. 誰 syīhwan 買東西？
4. 你想書上說的話都對嗎？
5. 我太太用多少錢買了一個房子？
6. 那個房子貴不貴？
7. 我問他甚麼？
8. 他爲甚麼要買那個房子？
9. 他爲甚麼買了很多的信紙？
10. 他買了一隻新筆，一個手表，———爲甚麼？

Ex. 13: CONTROLLED COMPOSITION. Rewrite paragraph 1 of the story, making the following changes. Switch men and women wherever they occur. Put the story in the negative. Write simplified characters where appropriate.

Ex. 14: CONTROLLED COMPOSITION.

Assume you are a married woman. You work teaching school. Your husband does not work. He is always out buying expensive things. One week he bought an expensive watch, the next an expensive pen, and the next a new house. Write a paragraph about this and his reasons for doing so.

Ex. 15: Each of the phrases listed below occurs in the story. Make a sentence using the phrase. You may model your sentences on the story, but do not copy the sentences from the story.

1. 甚麼時候用 ne ?
2. 有一回
3. 沒有人住
4. 這筆是新出來的
5. 誰都有

LESSON X

C. Review Exercises

Ex. 16: Write the Chinese equivalents beside the expressions.

now_____ breakfast_____ hear it said _____ why_____

eat_____ please be seated_____ able_____ things_____

know how to_____ may_____ only_____ think over_____

commerce, trade_____ use_____ that's right_____

time_____ give_____ come_____ good looking_____

how much_____ arrive here_____ in back_____

in front_____ what place?_____ parents_____ slow_____

inside the house_____ live, stay_____ quick_____

the first_____ therefore_____ last evening_____

sitting_____ wait a while_____

After completion, make a list of any characters in the sentences above that have simplified equivalents.

Ex. 17: SEEK AND FIND. Locate, circle, and write out the Chinese equivalent for the English items given below.

紙	好	五	紙	千	等	屋	紙
眞	千	女	房	信	萬	眞	子
人	五	新	屋	萬	誰	的	好
筆	表	眞	誰	兒	外	男	表
手	子	房	女	四	學	國	信
信	萬	萬	朋	生	屋	手	筆
友	房	信	人	男	房	信	眞
朋	常	很	寫	女	了	來	誰
女	誰	新	來	新	女	筆	女
男	常	筆	信	眞	常	手	男
常	紙	四	萬	萬	表	錶	紙

1. girl friend
2. men students
3. 400 million
4. house
5. who came?
6. really good
7. very new
8. letter paper
9. foreign pen
10. watch
11. write a letter
12. 5,000 people
13. frequently, often
14. daughter
15. room

Ex. 18: Rewrite the following sentences, replacing simplified characters with full characters and vice versa.

1. 谁买了新笔了？
2. 誰賣了兩萬本書？
3. 这信纸是从中国来的。
4. 他的父親送給他一隻新筆。
5. 那个房子是几万块钱买的？

THE CHARACTER BOOK: REVIEW LESSON B
(Lessons 6-10)
Exercises

Ex. 1: Write the following in Chinese numerals and read them aloud.

1. 86
2. $156.00
3. 6,523
4. $54.00
5. 9,999
6. $42,000.00
7. 38,561
8. $96,824.00
9. 75,446
10. $99,999.00
11. 87,917
12. $17,789.00
13. 91,877
14. $71,987.00
15. 18,719
16. $14,832.00
17. 56,634
18. $41,256.00
19. 82,588
20. $77,777.00

REVIEW LESSON B

Ex. 2:   Translate the following sentences into Chinese.

1. Please take the stationery into your room.

2. His parents have become old now.

3. Last Saturday, I couldn't talk with you because I had business to do.

4. Their son and daughter are both really good looking.

5. He gave me that very expensive wrist watch.

6. Listen! It's twelve o'clock at night now and those people are still talking.

7. They went from China to Japan last year.

8. Don't write with that pen. Why not use the new pen?

9. Last night they brought that large clock here.

10. Because Mr. Chyán (money) told us to come to school at 7:00, we got up at 6:00 this morning.

Ex. 3: Use each of the following phrases to make a sentence.

1. 到這兒

2. 從日本到中國

3. 從前年到明年

4. 從上星期到下個月

5. 從中國到 Dé 國

Ex. 4: Translate the following phrases into English.

1. 明天來

2. 昨天來

3. 前年去

4. 去年去

5. 明年念書

6. 現在不作買賣了

7. 常說中國話

8. 昨天就拿來了

9. 去年買的表太貴

10. 後年再來

REVIEW LESSON B

Ex. 5: Write the English equivalents of the Chinese expressions.

早 _____ 三點鐘 _____ 還是 _____ 住 _____

起來 _____ 新買的 _____ 姓錢 _____ 所 _____

家裏 _____ 門 _____ 房子 _____ 等一會兒 ___

兩塊 _____ 不知道 _____ 送給 _____

快 _____ 慢 _____

Ex. 6: Combine each of the characters in column A with each of those in column B to make phrases. Then add such characters as needed to make sentences.

    A 走   B 快
       寫   慢
       說   好
       念   不好
       學

Ex. 7: Translate the following into Chinese.

1. Take the large clock to the back (there).

2. Bring the books all out (here).

3. Pick up the clock.

4. Give the new house to him.

5. Give the $1,000.00 to him.

Ex. 8: Read the following numbers aloud and write them out in Arabic numerals.

1. 一千
2. 十一
3. 三千四百
4. 五萬
5. 九萬九千九百九十九
6. 一百十一
7. 八萬五千九百七十二
8. 六千四百
9. 四百五十六
10. 五萬七千八百四十二
11. 三萬三千八百二十九
12. 一萬九千二百一十六
13. 九萬五千一百七十六
14. 十五萬
15. 十九萬四千七百二十五
16. 一百萬
17. 三十一萬
18. 四十九萬八千五百
19. 六百四十萬
20. 一千萬

REVIEW LESSON B   145

Ex. 9:   SCRAMBLE/SEEK AND FIND. Snaking its way through
           the jumble of characters in the box below is the
           Chinese for 'My friend's father has 1,000 clocks,
           but his mother has only a small wristwatch. I
           have neither clock nor watch, nor money.' These
           are joined together without punctuation in a
           famous design often associated with China.

朋	屋	塊	了	門	位	年	母	情	昨	家	房	信	知
友	萬	明	又	禮	誰	出	父	塊	拜	父	位	千	道
父	男	昨	再	拜	從	親	家	新	屋	新	年	男	誰
母	女	晚	著	拿	我	沒	我	表	手	半	出	聽	千
沒	新	念	年	的	有	百	半	毛	千	小	把	愛	男
有	眞	現	朋	起	鐘	千	幾	出	筆	明	個	書	女
把	常	早	友	出	也	萬	點	等	紙	鐘	一	早	新
送	等	的	月	鐘	所	沒	聽	第	信	件	有	老	親
給	行	父	進	表	行	情	有	表	住	別	就	現	行
情	貴	親	愛	毛	太	知	現	念	也	禮	親	叫	送
事	著	還	有	手	因	道	老	今	沒	母	念	走	責
別	第	半	千	一	爲	快	門	書	有	他	今	老	從
件	所	意	萬	房	千	慢	表	錢	是	女	又	意	再
手	書	幾	男	件	出	個	鐘	可	再	眞	著	幾	手
表	老	走	女	道	今	姓	住	叫	快	常	晚	塊	表
住	爲	聽	思	姓	天	念	行	點	慢	屋	走	百	鐘

Ex. 10: Write the Chinese equivalents beside the English expressions.

this affair_____ stationery_____ ok?_____ now_____

again_____ reside_____ still_____ listen_____

order_____ week_____ house_____ how many?_____

new_____ truly_____ 1/2_____ to be surnamed_____

parents_____ know_____ this evening_____ study_____

therefore_____ because_____ very expensive_____

that gentleman (polite)_____ left hand_____

next year_____

Ex. 11: Translate the following phrases into Chinese.

1. the first book

2. one book

3. the 12th person

4. 12 people

5. the twenty-first year

6. twenty-one years

REVIEW LESSON B   147

Ex. 12: Translate the following sentences into Chinese.

1. The old man walked too slowly.

2. They brought the Chinese stationery.

3. Who is that woman surnamed Chyan (money)?

4. "Come in. Come in," said Mrs. Wang.

5. How much are these three pens?

6. They were very embarrassed.

7. Those books from Japan are still too expensive.

8. What is the meaning of this?

9. Don't go into the room. I want to bring the books out first.

10. They won't study tomorrow.

Ex. 13: Write the Yale romanization for the following characters and expressions.

現在_____ 叫_____ 千_____ 錢_____ 前_____

年_____ 念_____ 晚上_____ 第九_____

走了_____ 聽見_____ 是_____ 還是_____

女人_____ 母親_____ 別_____ 道_____

事_____ 十_____ 知_____ 姓_____

List here any simplified equivalents that occur in the above words.

Ex. 14: Cross Character Puzzle. Complete the following just as you would a crossword puzzle.

Down
2. I don't buy books often.
3. This letter paper is very good looking.
4. He loves to read Japanese books.
5. write a letter
6. daughter's study
7. really dull
8. new main door (gate)
9. last year

Across
1. see me off
3. This is a foreign pen.
4. He writes to (his) girl friend often.
7. really nice
11. to study
12. very new wrist watch
13. did not go to see the new house
14. outside the door

Ex. 15: Rewrite the following sentences, replacing simplified characters with full characters and vice versa.

1. 你什么时候从中国来?
2. 他們兩個都在後頭.
3. 请问现在九点钟吗?
4. 誰學寫中國字?
5. 纸, 笔, 书都贵, 对不对?
6. 你母親愛買東西嗎?

THE CHARACTER BOOK
LESSON XI

A. Exercises on Character Meaning and Use

Ex. 1: Draw lines connecting the English and Chinese expressions.

見	song
要緊	measure for sentence
一定	Jāng (surname) (simplified)
生气	Jāng (surname) (regular)
吧	must
歌	how, why
高	in midst of
句	important (simplified)
见	important (regular)
正	meet, see (simplified)
怎麼	meet, see (regular)
張	certainly
跟	with
唱	angry (simplified)
要	sing
呢	continuance of action (particle)
必	tall
张	suggestion, request (particle)
生氣	angry (regular)

LESSON XI   151

Ex. 2:   Place the letter beside the English meaning in
         the space beside the Chinese equivalent.

___ 正好   ___ 吧   ___ 唱歌   ___ 高   ___ 看見

___ 不必   ___ 見   ___ 生氣   ___ 一定   ___ 張

___ 怎麼   ___ 句   ___ 呢   ___ 跟   ___ 國歌

a. national anthem   h. how, why
b. visit   i. continuation (particle)
c. sentence classifier   j. sing
d. just right   k. with
e. flat classifier   l. tall
f. not necessary   m. see
g. suggestion (particle)   n. certainly
                              o. angry

Ex. 3:   Write the English equivalent beside the Chinese.

生氣 _____   張先生 _____   國歌 _____

怎麼 _____   正好 _____ 吧 _____   呢 _____

要緊 _____   看見 _____ 一定 _____   跟 _____

聽見 _____   高 _____   見 _____   正在看書 _____

跟著 _____   這句話 _____

Ex. 4:   Write the Chinese equivalent beside the English.

sing national anthem_____ get angry_____ tall_____

not gone yet_____ It must be this, isn't it?_____

be important_____ follow_____ see_____ visit_____

need not_____ how, why_____ certainly_____

continuation_____ is sitting_____ Mr. Jāng_____

hasn't gone yet_____ _____ two sentences_____

several sheets of letter paper (simp.)_____

very important (simp.)_____ air (simp.)_____

Ex. 5:   Translate into Chinese.

1. Is your friend tall?

2. I did not go to see Mr. Jāng.

3. He's very tall now.

4. Do you know how to sing the national anthem?

5. He said to me: "Don't get angry!"

LESSON XI

Ex. 6:   Translate into Chinese.

1. Mr. Gāu hasn't eaten yet.

2. Hasn't Mrs. Jāng eaten yet?

3. They're still studying.

4. Mrs. Jāng is in the midst of singing the national anthem.

5. Mr. and Mrs. Jāng still haven't gone to China yet.

Ex. 7:   Complete the following sentences with either 呢 or 了 and translate them into English.

1. 高先生正在吃飯 _____ 。
2. 張太太還沒好 _____ 。
3. 張先生的女兒現在很高 _____ 。
4. 高太太還作買賣 _____ 。
5. 我們還有筆 _____ 。
6. 我的兒子還不高 _____ 。
7. 你聽！<u>張必高</u>會說中文 _____ 。
8. 六點鐘 ___ ，你母親快要到 _____ 。
9. <u>張必高</u>現在在念書，不賣紙 _____ 。
10. 他還在唱歌 _____ 。

Ex. 8:   Translate into Chinese.

1. Formerly Mr. Jāng sold books and pens. Now he sells only books.

2. Last night they sang at Mrs. Gāu's home.

3. He's still angry.

4. When he returns, he will certainly be angry.

5. Are you still writing that one sentence?

Ex. 9:   Answer the following questions.

1. 那個人怎麼那麼高？
2. 那本書真有意思，你怎麼不想看？
3. 七點鐘了，張必高怎麼還沒來？
4. 你們明年怎麼去中國？
5. 那個字怎麼寫？

LESSON XI

Ex. 10: Complete these sentences by adding 吧 and translate them into English.

1. 吃飯＿＿。

2. 你兒子很高了＿＿？

3. 你說的那件事情很要緊＿＿。

4. 張先生六點鐘要回去＿＿。

5. 給你＿＿。

Ex. 11: Translate the following into Chinese and then use each of your translated phrases in a sentence.

1. that man in the midst of eating a meal

2. that very important matter

3. the song sung by Mr. Gāu

4. the very angry man in the room

5. the sentence written by Mr. Jāng

Ex. 12: Translate the following into Chinese.

1. How is it that you didn't go?

2. Mr. Jāng is still here singing.

3. These words--you needn't write them anymore.

4. The matter that you spoke of yesterday--that must be it, right?

5. What Mr. Gāu told you last night certainly must be important.

6. How is it that very angry man still hasn't left?

7. Mrs. Jāng still hasn't gone to Mr. Gāu's place yet.

After completing the above exercise, circle all characters which have simplified equivalents. Make sure that you can write each of them.

LESSON XI   157
              B.   Exercises on the Story

Ex. 13:   Answer the following questions.

1.   很有錢的那個人姓甚麼？
2.   他愛作甚麼？
3.   張先生唱的歌兒好不好聽？
4.   要是有人說他唱的歌兒好聽，張先生就作甚麼？
5.   老 Lǐ 聽說甚麼？
6.   老 Lǐ 為甚麼去見張先生？
7.   老 Lǐ 對張先生說甚麼？
8.   第二天老 Lǐ 又到哪兒去了？
9.   張先生為甚麼給老 Lǐ 五塊錢？
10.   老 Lǐ 為甚麼把五塊錢還 (hwán-return) 給張先生？

Ex. 14:   CONTROLLED COMPOSITION.

There is an American living in China who has studied some Chinese. He loves to talk Chinese with other people and (typical of Americans!?) pays people who say he speaks well. A Frenchman who speaks Chinese very well decides to go get some of the free money. He hears the American speak Chinese and says with surprise that it is quite good. The American gives him $10.00, but because the American's Chinese really is good, the Frenchman returns it.

Write a short essay on this story.

Ex. 15:   Below is a translation of paragraphs 1 and 4 of the story. Without looking at the book, translate them back into Chinese and then check your work against the book.

   There was a very rich man surnamed Jāng. He really liked to sing. He didn't sing too well; but he thought that other people definitely all liked to hear the songs he sang. He frequently asked other people to listen to him sing, (and if) there was (a) person saying his songs were sung well, he then gave that person money.

   Mr. Jāng said: 'Yesterday I learned another song. I'll sing it once and you have a listen.' He then sang again. He sang one sentence, (while) still in the midst of happily singing, Old Li said: 'Sir, I'd better give you your $5.00. The song you're singing still isn't good to listen to.'

LESSON XI

C. Exercise on Character Shape and Origin

Ex. 16: The characters in each group below all share a common component. Add to each group those characters in Lesson 11 which share the same component.

1. 愛　念　思　意
2. 知　叫　吃　問
3. 寫　字
4. 親　看

D. Review Exercises

Ex. 17: Write the Chinese equivalents beside the English expressions.

man_____ new_____ 6,000 people_____ must_____

how_____ send, deliver_____ because_____ love____

come in_____ don't_____ sing_____ become angry_____

a sentence_____ important_____ know_____ wait_____

back door_____ from_____ fast_____ slow_____ again_____

too much_____ meaning_____ ok or not?_____ study_____

tomorrow_____ evening_____ now_____

Ex. 18: Complete the following sentences.

1. 我把張先生那個大鐘 _____

2. 老高一到家了就_____

3. 張先生張太太爲甚麼_____

4. 學生們怎麼_____

5. 因爲我們星期二不必上學，所以 _____

6. 張先生送我_____

7. 我去見張先生，可是我到的時候他正在_____

8. 請你給高太太_____

9. 很貴的書不一定都_____

10. 男女都_____

LESSON XI   161

Ex. 19: Cross Character Puzzle. Complete the following
        just as you would a crossword puzzle.

Down
2. And him?
3. Mr. Jāng doesn't know how to sing (song).
4. important words (spoken)
5. I and you
8. one sentence
9. national anthem

Across
1. (How about) give him several sheets of letter paper.
6. He will be angry, I suppose.
7. You certainly know how to speak Chinese.
10. to talk

Ex. 20: Rewrite the following sentences, replacing simplified characters with full characters and vice versa.

1. 为什么张先生不唱国歌?
2. 因為他生氣了，所以他不吃飯.
3. 不要紧的话，一句都不必说.
4. 我想沒聽見也不要緊吧?
5. 张先生不要见他，他就生气了.

THE CHARACTER BOOK
LESSON XII

A. Exercises on Character Meaning and Use

Ex. 1: Draw lines connecting the Chinese and English expressions.

弟弟	forgot
懂	white
孩子	forget
站	already (simplified)
差不多	already (regular)
岁	stand
城	child
已	daytime
白	tell (simplified)
難	younger brother
告訴	night time
忘	approximately
已經	difficult (simplified)
夜裏	city
歲	understand
白天	difficult (regular)
忘了	years of age (simplified)
告诉	years of age (regular)
难	tell (regular)

163

Ex. 2: Place the letter of the English meaning in the space beside its Chinese equivalent.

已經____ 三弟____ 沒忘____ 難看____ 站起來____

差不多____ 幾歲了____ 站____ 一夜____ 明白____

白紙____ 很難懂____ 告訴____ 城裏____ 女孩子____

a. understand
b. one night
c. didn't forget
d. third younger brother
e. tell
f. stand up
g. white paper
h. how old (are you)?
i. ugly
j. already
k. almost
l. hard to understand
m. station, depot
n. in the city
o. girl

Ex. 3: In the blanks, write the English equivalents of the Chinese expressions.

白紙____   難吃____   站起來____

不懂____   沒告訴____   小孩子____

弟弟____   出城____   已經____

差一塊錢____   別告訴他____

早已經吃了____   半夜____

進城____   男孩子____   差不多____

真難____   差十 fēn 十二點____

LESSON XII

Ex. 4: In the blanks, write the Chinese equivalents for the English expressions.

already_____ almost, about_____ have forgotten_____

white_____ difficult_____ stand up_____ tall_____

younger brother_____ inside the city_____

one night_____ how old are (you)?_____

understand_____ ugly_____ child_____ girl_____

go out of the city_____ unpalatable (simp.)_____

already came (simp.)_____ years of age (simp.)_____

Ex. 5: Translate the following sentences into Chinese.

1. They have already left.

2. They had already come day before yesterday.

3. He is already here.

4. Are you already 9 years old?

5. That book is rather hard to understand. I have already read it five times.

Ex. 6: Translate each of the following phrases into Chinese, and use each of your phrases in a sentence.

1. the very tall boy
2. reside in the city
3. the girl who is seven years old
4. that forty-year old woman
5. ten minutes to one
6. really hard to understand
7. the book I forgot to buy
8. twenty minutes to six
9. almost thirty years old
10. fourth younger brother

Ex. 7: Translate the following sentences into Chinese.

1. That old man really loves to sing at night.
2. That small child is their tenth younger brother.
3. Tomorrow I must go out of the city to see a friend.
4. Don't tell him I'm going to give him a new book.
5. The food she cooks is really unpalatable.
6. Mr. Jāng stood up, said 'thank you,' and left.
7. They don't study during the daytime.
8. My daughter is already five years old.
9. One night I heard him speak Chinese.
10. He ate long ago.

LESSON XII

Ex. 8: Combine each of the expressions in column A with as many of those in column B as possible. Translate the combinations that you make.

A	B
城	外頭
幾	裏
白	看
夜	歲
難	懂
差	紙
很	不多

Ex. 9: Rewrite these sentences in the negative.

1. 張先生，張太太已經來了。

2. 我們的先生寫的那本書很難懂。

3. Wáng先生已經九十歲了。

4. 昨天夜裏我們忘了告訴你們。

5. 男孩子都已經站起來了。

Ex. 10: Complete these sentences with expressions from Lesson 12.

1. 他們有兩個 ___ ___ 大的七 ___，小的六 ___。

2. 昨天 ___ ___ 張太太沒 ___ ___ 我這件事情。

3. 我有一個 ___ ___ 他已經三 ___ 了。

4. 先生說的中國話，我們 ___ ___ ___ 都不 ___。

5. 我真不 ___ ___ 你為什麼不學中文。

6. 差 ___ ___ 兒。

7. 不知道，早 ___ ___ ___ 了。

8. Wáng 正國！不要 ___ ___ 吃飯去。

9. ___ ___ 有一個小學。

10. Wáng 正國在 hwǒchē ___ ___ 吃飯。

LESSON XII   169

Ex. 11:   Translate the following into English.

1. 張太太昨天夜裏就已經到了。
2. 學生們都在 hwǒchē 站等先生來。
3. 那個男孩子說他不懂，可是我想這本書不太難懂。
4. 城裏沒有大學。
5. 五弟今年四歲了。
6. 我不明白我為甚麼差兩塊錢。
7. Wáng 小 jye 前天沒告訴張太太嗎？
8. 這個女孩子很好看，你為甚麼說他難看？
9. 我忘了站起來。
10. 那些小孩子差不多都會唱中國國歌兒。

Ex. 12: SEEK AND FIND. Circle and write out the Chinese equivalents of the expressions listed below.

1. tell
2. very hard to understand
3. didn't forget
4. ugly
5. younger brother
6. how old (are you)?
7. midnight
8. boy
9. inside the city
10. already
11. have forgotten
12. stand up
13. one night
14. seven years old
15. daytime

忙	機	的	看	必	沒
了	幾	大	不	忘	高
自	歲	子	了	第	田
巳	了	跟	白	第	力
給	成	天	張	巳	子
城	裏	告	經	緊	看
裏	訴	那	要	難	見
頭	以	弟	歲	七	半
站	眞	弟	懂	男	夜
七	起	吧	難	孩	一
來	了	來	很	子	怎

LESSON XII   171

B. Exercises on the Story

Ex. 13: Answer the following questions on the story.

1. 那個小孩子姓甚麼，叫甚麼 míng 字？

2. 他幾歲了？

3. 高明眞甚麼都會，對不對？

4. 高明眞在哪兒上學？

5. 他念了一天的書，第二天爲甚麼先生問他甚麼，他都不知道？

6. 先生問明眞甚麼？

7. 中國一 gùng 有多少人？

8. 明眞說中國有多少人？

9. 他說的對不對？

10. 學 syàu 裏的先生都 syǐhwan 高明眞嗎？

Ex. 14: Below is an English version of the first paragraph of the story. Translate it back into Chinese, and check your version against the original.

There was a child surnamed Gāu, with the name of Míng-jēn. He had already reached eight years of age, but he still understood nothing. He went to a school in the city, and by night he forgot all that he had studied during the day. The next day (when he) got into school whatever his teacher would ask him, he didn't know. Therefore, almost all his teachers did not like him.

Ex. 15: CONTROLLED COMPOSITION. Rewrite paragraph two of the story, making these changes. The hero is 高沒用. The place is America, and the population discussed is American.

Ex. 16: CONTROLLED COMPOSITION.

Write a paragraph about 張正國. He is a student in a middle school outside the city. He is already 13 years old and doesn't like school. He studies all day, understands everything, and doesn't forget anything. He thinks that school is not very hard, and yesterday he told that to his teacher. Today, he no longer attends school.

LESSON XII   173

C. Review Exercises

Ex. 17: Translate the following sentences into Chinese.

1. They didn't come last night. They'll come tomorrow.

2. He wasn't at school yesterday.

3. That little girl wants my younger brother to give her a book.

4. Mr. Bái saw Mr. Gāu yesterday in the city.

5. Why is it they still haven't come yet?

6. Who bought the new house outside of town?

7. How can I write a letter? I have neither stationery nor pen.

8. Mr. Bái doesn't often sing foreign songs.

9. This clock is my friend's clock.

10. You've become so tall. How old are you now?

11. The first year that I studied in China I lived at school.

12. What is the surname of that lovely girl we saw yesterday in the city?

13. What time do you get up in the morning?

14. Mr. Gāu often eats at home.

15. The teacher said to the students, "I'll wait for you at school."

16. Chinese food is really good to eat, but foreign food is usually unpalatable.

17. I don't understand anything you say. I've forgotten all the Chinese I studied.

18. They've already written almost ten books.

19. That seven-year-old girl has left already.

20. I told him, "The watch was very expensive."

After completing the above translation, scan all twenty sentences and circle any character that has a simplified equivalent. Make sure you can write all of them.

THE CHARACTER BOOK
LESSON XIII

A. Exercises on Character Meaning and Use

Ex. 1: Draw lines connecting the Chinese and English expressions.

賣報的	water
謝謝	close (simplified)
跑	newspaper seller
開	pass (simplified)
车	come over here
一分錢	look for
过	run
十五分鐘	15 minutes
关	open (simplified)
過來	open (regular)
教書	teach
火	cent
开	pass (regular)
水	vehicle (simplified)
關	school
學校	fire
過	must
必得	close (regular)
車	thanks
找	vehicle (regular)

Ex. 2: Place the letter of the English meaning in the space beside the Chinese equivalent.

____不謝 ____找房子 ____關門 ____火車站

____七點過五分 ____看報 ____開門 ____找人

____兩分鐘 ____教我寫字 ____三點三刻

____快跑 ____買報 ____過去 ____關着呢

a. two minutes
b. close the door
c. buy newspapers
d. (is) closed
e. look for a house
f. quickly run
g. read a newspaper
h. teach me to write
i. 3:45
j. train station
k. open the door
l. 7:05
m. look for someone
n. go over (there)
o. no need to thank

Ex. 3: Write the English equivalent beside the Chinese expression.

多謝 _____ 一定得買 _____ 過 _____

水 _____ 上車 _____ 報 _____ 火 _____

跑得很快 _____ 四分錢 _____

九點三刻 _____ 車開了 _____ 教書 _____

謝謝 _____ 找房子 _____ 十一點一刻 _____

LESSON XIII

Ex. 4: Write the Chinese equivalents beside the English expressions.

water_____ fire_____ vehicle_____ newspaper_____

school_____ open_____ close_____ cent_____ teach_____

look for_____ thank_____ run_____ must_____ cross_____

open the door_____ teach_____ train_____ school_____

sell papers_____ 3:45_____ 7:05 (simp.)_____

get out of a car (simp.)_____ close the door (simp.)_____

Ex. 5: Translate the following phrases into Chinese.

1. runs fast
2. runs very fast
3. eats slowly
4. doesn't run fast
5. teaches very well
6. sings very badly
7. doesn't study too rapidly
8. walks slowly
9. learns slowly
10. speaks very well

Ex. 6: Make us a sentence with each of the phrases in Ex. 5. Remember that when an object follows the verb, the verb must be repeated before the adverb. For this exercise, write your sentences in simplified characters.

Ex. 7: Translate the following into English.

1. 火車還沒有到呢。
2. 學校裏有人在跑嗎？
3. 張先生是一個敎書的。
4. 賣報的叫我們別跑得太快。
5. 他關門。我開門。他又把門關上了。
6. 你說的是幾點鐘？三點三刻，還是三點三分？
7. 這個水不好 hē 。
8. 他們找甚麼房子？
9. 學生們爲甚麼沒說「謝謝」？
10. Wáng 太太要孩子們過來。

LESSON XIII

Ex. 8:   Translate the following into Chinese.

1. Whom are you looking for?

2. Run quickly!!

3. Pardon me. I must go.

4. He invited me to go over there.

5. The door is closed. Who will open it?

6. The train will come at 4:45.

7. I said, 'many thanks' to him, but he said, 'Don't thank (me).'

8. The newspaper seller sells in front of the school.

9. Please teach me to write Chinese characters.

10. He told me to drink some water.

Ex. 9:   Translate the following phrases and sentences into Chinese. Note that they call for the use of the 'experiential' gwò. 過

1. have never gone to China

2. have read that book (before)

3. have spoken Chinese with him (before)

4. have never eaten foreign food

5. have read today's newspaper

6. Have you ever been to China?

7. They say they have all read the book.

8. We've never spoken Chinese with him.

9. Have the students ever eaten Chinese food?

10. I still haven't seen him.

Ex. 10: Fill in the blanks in the following sentences with expressions from Lesson 13. Translate the sentences into English.

1. 學＿＿＿大門怎麼還沒＿＿＿呢？
2. 我跟 Wáng 先生說＿＿＿＿＿ ＿＿＿＿＿。
3. 對不起，我現在＿＿＿＿走。
4. 昨天他沒有跟我說話，因為他＿＿＿到城裏去＿＿＿房子。
5. ＿＿＿ ＿＿＿走的太慢．
6. ＿＿＿ ＿＿＿一到上海， Wáng 先生就＿＿＿ ＿＿＿了。
7. 我請 Wáng 先生＿＿＿我寫中國字。
8. 我們都沒去＿＿＿他們那裏。
9. 小張沒用，學＿＿＿中文，可是他都忘了。
10. "我＿＿＿＿＿進去，請他快＿＿＿門!!"

LESSON XIIII 181

Ex. 11: Use each of the following expressions in a sentence. Note that they may be made affirmative or negative. The objects are left for you to supply.

1. 過去
2. 過來
3. 跑過去
4. 看過
5. 吃過
6. 走過去
7. 寫過
8. 說過
9. 學過
10. 問過

B. Exercises on the Story

Ex. 12: Answer the following questions on the story.

1. 那四位教書先生在哪兒等火車？
2. 他們在那兒作甚麼？
3. 誰說話說得很高興？
4. 到 Nyǒuywē 去的火車甚麼時候開？
5. 現在是甚麼時候？
6. 那位老先生去找甚麼？
7. 那三位老先生為甚麼沒看見火車來了？
8. 那三位老先生為甚麼上火車了？
9. 有一個人說不要緊，為甚麼？
10. 那四位老先生，幾位要走，幾位不走？

Ex. 13: The following paragraphs are translated from the story. Translate them back into Chinese, and check your translation against the original.

Later on, the person at the station (the station attendant) saw him, and (then) said to him, 'Sir, this is not important. Of the four of you, haven't three of you already gone on board(?), and only you alone haven't gone. You can take the next train.

He said, 'You don't know!! It was only me who needed to go. The three of them all came to see me off.'

Ex. 14: CONTROLLED COMPOSITION. Rewrite paragraphs one and two of the story, changing the number of people into eight, the time into night, and their occupations into newspaper sellers.

Ex. 15: CONTROLLED COMPOSITION. Write one paragraph about you and three friends waiting for a train. The train was to have come at 3:15 but you waited and waited and it didn't come. By 4:30 it still had not yet come. You asked someone at the station why it did not come, and he said that it left yesterday.

LESSON XIII

C. Exercise on Character Shape and Origin

Ex. 16: Identify and circle the common component in each of the following groups of characters, and suggest a principle that might have underlain the makeup of these characters.

1. 門　問　開　關

2. 找　我　把

3. 刻　分　別

4. 過　進　送　這　還

D. Review Exercises

Ex. 17: Give the English equivalents beside the Chinese expressions.

已經 _____   難看 _____

弟弟 _____   必得 _____   要緊 _____

怎麼 _____   生氣 _____   唱歌 _____

屋子 _____   中國筆 _____   愛 _____

貴 _____   慢 _____   等 _____   出 _____

知道 _____   年 _____   住 _____   姓 _____

家裏 _____   一點兒 _____   還沒有 _____

早來 _____   所以 _____   為甚麼 _____

Ex. 18: Translate the following paragraph into Chinese.

    I have an old friend surnamed Jāng. He is a very good person. When we were in school, he was a very good student and studied well. In high school and college he studied Chinese. Now he is in China doing business. But he also still studies Chinese. He says that because he studied Chinese in school he is now able to do business in China, and because he does business in China, he is still able to study Chinese.

LESSON XIII

Ex. 19: Cross Character Puzzle. Complete the following just like a crossword puzzle.

Down
1. the schools in the city
2. almost
3. my younger brother's
4. thanks to the newspaper seller
5. board a train or car
6. railway station
7. walk over here
8. run quickly

Across
6. The train goes very fast.
9. teach me
10. inside
11. don't thank (me)
12. many thanks
13. student
14. water seller
15. drive a car
16. come to look for a person

Ex. 20: Rewrite the following sentences, replacing simplified characters with full characters and vice versa.

1. 火车站里头的卖报的还沒来呢。
2. 我給了那個孩子五塊錢，他說："謝謝！"
3. 现在已经八点过十分了。
4. 還有一刻鐘火車就開了。
5. 学校的大门关着呢。

THE CHARACTER BOOK
LESSON XIV

A. Exercises on Character Meaning and Use

Ex. 1: Draw lines connecting the Chinese and English equivalents.

打算	recognize
自己	put down
茶	smile
認得	underneath
放	be acquainted with (simplified)
放下	hit
上街	free time
底下	oneself
菜	vegetables
笑	tea
认识	table
大街	main street
工夫	plan to
桌子	let go of, put, place
打	be acquainted with (regular)
認識	go to the shopping district

Ex. 2: Write the number of the English equivalent beside the Chinese expression.

___ 笑 ___ 底下 ___ 自己 ___ 書桌 ___ 作菜

___ 茶 ___ 打 ___ 認得 ___ 打算 ___ 沒工夫卖

___ 放 ___ 街 ___ 放下 ___ 认识 ___ 工夫

a. recognize
b. put, place
c. smile
d. below
e. hit
f. no time to sell
g. plan to
h. street

i. be acquainted be
j. cook dishes
k. desk
l. oneself
m. tea
n. leisure time
o. put down

Ex. 3: Write the English equivalent beside the Chinese expression.

放下 _____ 自己 _____ 認識 _____

作菜 _____ 桌子 _____ 工夫 _____

茶 _____   打算 _____ 笑 _____

上街 _____ 底下 _____ 放下 _____

打 _____   認得 _____ 笑話 _____

LESSON XIV   189

Ex. 4:   Write the Chinese equivalent beside the English
         expression.

recognize_____ put_____ laugh_____ main street_____

slow_____ free time_____ myself_____ table_____

vegetables_____ tea_____ put down_____ plan_____

smile_____ leisure time_____ dish of food_____

go to the shopping district_____ hit_____

desk_____ himself_____ herself_____ Chinese tea____

be acquainted with (simplified)_____

Ex. 5:   Use expressions in column A to combine with those
         in column B to make as many phrases as you can.
         Translate the phrases you make into English.

	A 作	B 高先生
	中國	茶
	外國	自己
	好吃的	話
	我	菜
	他們	
	認識	
	笑	

Ex. 6:   Translate the following into English.

1. 張太太是誰？我不認識他。
2. 請你放在棹子上。
3. Wáng 先生那麼老，他怎麼自己作菜呢？
4. 張大明笑着說：「我今天夜裏兩點鐘打算上街。」
5. 請你看看，底下有白紙沒有？
6. 對不起！！我們今天沒有工夫，不能跟你一塊兒去。
7. 棹子上的茶好 hē 嗎？
8. 他爲甚麼常自己跟自己說話？
9. 街上有沒有茶 gwǎn 兒？
10. 我昨天不是說笑話，我眞打算去中國。

LESSON XIV

Ex. 7: Fill in the blanks with words from Lesson 14.

1. 我不 ___ ___ 他，他是誰？
2. 那張___子很大，你為甚麼不把東西___在桌子上呢？
3. 他常常___話，我有___ ___，很想去聽聽。
4. 你找的那本書不在____子上嗎？你再看___下吧。
5. ___子上的那些中國___是誰的？
6. 他 ___ ___ 說：「他不會說中國話。」
7. 這個好吃的____是誰作的？
8. 他母親上___買東西去了。
9. 高太太明年 ___ ___ 上大學。
10. 張小明常說 "別___我"，可是沒有人要笑他。

Ex. 8:   Complete the following sentences. Each of your completions should include some characters from Lesson 14.

1. 我昨天找不到的表，你 ＿＿＿＿＿＿＿＿＿＿＿。
2. 他們明年 ＿＿＿＿＿＿＿＿＿＿＿。
3. 你甚麼時候有＿＿＿＿＿，我請你吃飯。
4. 我們是老朋友，你 ＿＿＿＿＿＿＿＿＿。
5. 他作的菜很多，可是他說 ＿＿＿＿＿＿＿＿＿。
6. 那位老先生常 ＿＿＿＿＿＿＿＿＿。
7. 我天天 ＿＿＿＿＿＿＿＿＿。
8. 這個東西你要我 ＿＿＿＿＿＿＿＿＿。
9. 我還不知道我學甚麼，你 ＿＿＿＿＿＿＿＿＿。
10. 他是誰，我不 ＿＿＿＿＿＿＿＿＿。

LESSON XIV

Ex. 9: Translate the following into Chinese.

1. Where did you put my clock?

2. Do you have free time next Thursday?

3. I don't know even a single Japanese.

4. Is there a restaurant on Main Street?

5. Are there tables below?

6. Do they sell Chinese tea?

7. I'll sell my car myself.

8. What dishes did you order?

9. When did he himself say he was going?

10. Tomorrow I don't plan on going to school.

Ex. 10: Translate using simplified characters.

1. Where did you put the clock that I bought yesterday?

2. Do you have free time day after tomorrow?

3. I myself hit the man who works in the train station.

4. The restaurant on Main Street is very good.

5. The tables below are too small.

6. The Chinese tea that they sell is too expensive.

7. The cars that he himself sells are not too expensive.

8. The dishes that you ordered are all good to eat.

9. He said he was going at 2:45.

10. The school that I go to is on first street.

LESSON XIV

B. Exercises on the Story

Ex. 11: Answer the following questions on the story.

1. 那一天差不多幾點鐘我ě了？
2. 我打算到哪兒去？
3. 飯gwǎn兒都開着嗎？
4. 因為飯gwǎn兒沒開，所以我到甚麼地方去了？
5. Jyǒugwǎn兒裏有沒有桌子？
6. 誰找了一張桌子就坐下了？
7. 「要了一個菜」Yīngwén (=English) 怎麼說？
8. 我要了些甚麼東西？
9. Jyǒugwǎn兒裏的人多不多？我認識他們嗎？
10. 有幾個人站在一塊兒作甚麼？
11. 「賣jyǒu的給他一伺jyǒu，拿一伺錢」Yīngwén 怎麼說？
12. 有一個人跟誰說話？
13. 我為甚麼jywé得那個人很tè別？
14. 我過去問那個人甚麼？
15. 你念了這個gù事，就笑了—— 對不對？

Ex. 12: The following is an English version of the first paragraph of the story. Translate it back into Chinese and compare your translation with the original.

(It was) one night, somewhat past one. I became hungry. Originally, I planned to go to a restaurant to eat something, but it was too late, and the restaurants were all closed. On the street there was a bar that was still open. I then went to that bar.

Ex. 13: CONTROLLED COMPOSITION. Write a couple of paragraphs on the following situation. <u>Do not translate.</u>

One night about 1:30 you got hungry. Because all the restaurants were closed, you went to your Chinese teacher's house. Your Chinese teacher is a famous cook, and you knew you could get something good to eat. But he was not at home. At last you went to a bar, and there he was drinking and talking with himself. You listened to him for one half hour and laughed. What was he saying?? (You finish the story.)

Ex. 14: CONTROLLED COMPOSITION. Write a paragraph about going to a restaurant. You ordered rice, one dish and tea. The waiter said that the dishes and tea were all gone (都沒有了). So you finally ordered rice and wine.

LESSON XIV

C. Review Exercises

Ex. 15: Write the Chinese equivalents beside the English terms.

look for_____ run quickly_____ understand_____

close the door_____ already_____ tell____ forget____

year of age_____ younger brother_____ certainly_____

tall_____ with, and _____ see_____ sing songs_____

get angry_____ female_____ male____ really good_____

often_____ who_____ pen_____ deliver_____ week_____

love_____ enter_____ affair_____ other_____ know_____

year_____ door_____

Ex. 16: Translate the following into Chinese.

   Last night I was very busy. I read two books. I wrote a lot of Chinese characters. I sold my car. I wrote a letter to my boyfriend. At one o'clock I got hungry, but there was no food in the house to eat. Finally, I ate my Chinese book. It was delicious!

Ex. 17: Seek and Find. Circle and write out the Chinese equivalents of the expressions listed below.

大	工	識	買	放	算	街	識
自	街	放	菜	茶	認	放	打
棹	大	笑	自	底	自	算	得
己	算	打	認	大	別	笑	我
菜	棹	下	棹	識	己	底	笑
子	街	底	己	上	棹	菜	作
茶	認	夫	話	下	茶	識	子
夫	上	放	已	笑	得	夫	上
街	工	要	自	認	子	笑	下
打	菜	底	街	工	要	放	工

1. self
2. table
3. cook dishes
4. buy tea
5. free time
6. plan to
7. main street
8. be acquainted with
9. put down
10. joke
11. underneath
12. recognize
13. go to the shopping district
14. don't laugh at me
15. order (in a restaurant)

Ex. 18: Rewrite the following sentences, replacing simplified characters with full characters and vice versa.

1. 你还认得那个地方吗?
2. 他說他不認識謝先生.
3. 张先生谁都认识.
4. 你認得我弟弟嗎?
5. 他们两个都认识钱先生吧!

THE CHARACTER BOOK
LESSON XV

A. Exercises on Character Meaning and Use

Ex. 1: Draw lines connecting the English and Chinese equivalents.

哥　　　　　elder brother
病　　　　　become sick
帮　　　　　willing to (simplified)
睡　　　　　willing to (regular)
願意　　　　cry
應當　　　　play
喜歡　　　　help (simplified)
哭　　　　　help (regular)
愿意　　　　sick
玩兒　　　　like (simplified)
够了　　　　like (regular)
平常　　　　sufficient
帶　　　　　ordinarily
喜欢　　　　carry, take (simplified)
路　　　　　carry, take (regular)
幫　　　　　road
带　　　　　sleep
愛哭　　　　should (simplified)
应当　　　　should (regular)
病了　　　　love to cry

LESSON XV

Ex. 2: Write the letter of the English equivalent beside the Chinese expression.

a. sick person
b. help me
c. like
d. walk
e. should
f. not enough
g. main road
h. don't cry
i. didn't sleep well
j. on the road
k. elder brother
l. play for awhile
m. help
n. bring money along
o. peaceful

___ 哥哥 ___ 喜歡 ___ 病人 ___ 走路

___ 玩兒一會兒 ___ 別哭 ___ 幫

___ 路上 ___ 睡的不好 ___ 平ān

___ 应当 ___ 大路 ___ 不够

___ 帶錢 ___ 幫我

Ex. 3: Write the English equivalents beside the Chinese expressions.

路 _____ 大哥 _____ 睡 jyàu _____

有病 _____ 願意 _____ 不喜歡 _____

帶我去 _____ 平常 _____ 玩兒 _____

哭 _____ 應當 _____ 不够 _____

幫 jù _____ 告訴 _____ 礼拜 _____

Ex. 4: Write the Chinese equivalents beside the English expressions.

should _____ enough _____ meaning _____ take _____

like to _____ road _____ help out _____ sleep _____

elder brother _____ should _____ sick _____ cry _____

willing to _____ peaceful _____ ordinarily _____

wish to _____ become sick _____ sleep _____ play _____

should come (simp.) _____ bring money (simp.) _____

help me do this (simp.) _____ 10,000 _____

LESSON XV

Ex. 5:   Translate into English.

1. 我很喜歡跟他一塊兒上街買東西去。

2. 他今天沒來因爲他昨天晚上病了。

3. 你昨晚爲甚麼睡得不好？

4. 我不能買那本書，因爲錢不够。

5. 我母親不願意帶我去。

6. 學生平常不願意說中國話。

7. 我弟弟說他不喜歡哭，可是他眞愛哭。

8. 你哥哥自己應當去見他。

9. 請你幫我寫這個字。

10. 他病的時候，他一定哭。

Ex. 6:   Translate into English.

1. 你哥哥昨天晚上來了，可是我不在家。
2. 有一個小男孩在路上玩。
3. 他們說他們願意把孩子帶走。
4. 先生叫我們不要帶書。
5. 你喜歡在早上玩兒嗎？
6. 他們應當明天早上去。
7. 平常我的錢不夠。
8. 我不知道為甚麼我昨天夜裏睡得不好。
9. 你願意幫 ju 他們嗎？
10. 老太太說他們去年病了。

LESSON XV

Ex. 7:   Translate into Chinese.

1. They should have left already.

2. Last night he said he liked to play with them.

3. The teacher said we should help our friends.

4. They didn't like the Chinese tea which we gave them yesterday.

5. Year before last, they weren't willing to attend school.

6. When they hit my elder brother, he was on the road.

7. She didn't help me last night.

8. Last week we didn't have any money to buy the pens.

9. You should bring more money.

10. My eldest brother does not like to talk.

Ex. 8: Translate into Chinese. (in simplified characters)

1. The one that I wanted to buy was too expensive.

2. The ones that he liked weren't in the store.

3. The road they went on was the highway.

4. The man you helped is my older brother.

5. The people he likes are all tall.

6. The child who was playing at school last night is my younger brother.

7. That old man without enough money is Mr. Gāu.

8. Those who brought their children along were school teachers.

9. The young lady who was sick last night came to my house today.

10. Those children who ordinarily don't cry are my students.

LESSON XV   207

Ex. 9:   Translate these phrases into Chinese, and make
         a sentence with each of your phrases.

1. didn't hit me   6. weren't sick
2. didn't sleep last night   7. hasn't fallen asleep
3. when I met them   8. didn't like him last year
4. hasn't yet cried   9. wasn't willing to help
5. wasn't willing to   10. didn't play

Ex. 10: Complete the following sentences. In your comple-
         tions use characters from lesson 15.

1. 我現在 _____。
2. 那個孩子!! 他真 _____。
3. Wáng 先生很有錢可是張先生 _____。
4. 他們的父母說他們 _____。
5. 昨天夜裏十一點鐘有一個朋友來找我 _____。
6. 我沒有工夫，可是他不 _____。
7. 他想跑過來，可是我 _____。
8. 你們爲甚麼沒 _____？
9. 張先生甚麼時候 _____？
10. 弟弟對 _____。

Ex. 12:   The following paragraphs come from the story. Translate them back into Chinese and compare your translation with the original.

  Mr. and Mrs. Lǐ have no children. They told me to live in their home. They liked me very much, (and) were truly very good to me.
  When I was fiye, (I) began school. Every day in the morning, Mrs. Lǐ called me to get up, cooked breakfast for me, and delivered me to school. When I finished classes, after I got home, they always asked me what I wanted to eat (and) what I wanted to play. Each day, before I slept, they told me a story.
  Later on I grew up. I often thought, (well) now they've become old. They have a lot of things to do, (and) I should help them do their business. Therefore (although) many times my friends told me I should go elsewhere to study, I never went. I thought I should still live together with them.

Ex. 13:   CONTROLLED COMPOSITION. Write a paragraph about yourself. You have reached 21. Your parents are old, and you think you should stay with them. They, however, urge you to go elsewhere to study. You figure that they are not ill and are still not too old, so you say you'll go. They give you $1,000.00 for spending money when you leave. They send you off at the railroad station crying.

LESSON XV

Ex. 14: CONTROLLED COMPOSITION. Write a paragraph about your first week away from home at college. Everyday your mother writes you a letter, and every day you write one to her. When she reads your letters, she cries, and when you read her letters, you cry. You do not like school. You always think of your home, and you plan to return home quickly. But suddenly you meet a girl/boy. You like her/him very much. Now you no longer write every day to your mother, but once per week. She still writes once a day. She cries when she reads your letters. She also cries when you don't write her.

Ex. 15: CONTROLLED COMPOSITION. Write a paragraph about when you were young. Your parents were very good to you. When you reached five, you began school. Every morning, your mother got you up, cooked breakfast, and sent you off to school When you came home, your parents would read stories to you and play with you. Because you now are away from home at college, you constantly think of your parents and when you were young.

B. Exercises on the Story

Ex. 11: Answer the following questions on the story.

1. 我是甚麼時候跟那位老先生說的話？
2. 他跟我說甚麼？
3. 他姓甚麼？
4. 那位老人小的時候，他家有些甚麼人？
5. Lǐ 先生是誰？
6. Lǐ 先生 Lǐ 太太叫「我」作甚麼？
7. 我五歲的時候，我天天作甚麼？
8. 誰給我作早飯？ 誰送我上學？
9. 我大了的時候，我常常作甚麼？
10. 我的朋友叫我去作甚麼？
11. 我二十五歲的時候， Lǐ 先生叫我作甚麼？
12. 我沒走以前，他們送給我甚麼？
13. 他們送我到火車站的時候，他們作甚麼？
14. 我為甚麼回去了？
15. 你想我回去是對還是不對？

LESSON XV

C. Review Exercises

Ex. 16: Translate into Chinese.

1. 2,563

2. How much money do you have?

3. He said to me, "When did you buy that car?"

4. A good many people like to study Chinese.

5. He plans to return to America next year.

6. 9,678

7. My friend is in school studying.

8. That old man still hasn't heard what I said.

9. Why are you leaving now?

10. How old is your young son?

11. My younger brother still lives at home with my parents.

12. Last evening someone named Jāng came to see you.

13. The house that they live at is too large.

14. I know that the clock in front of the main gate is fast.

Ex. 16: Continued.

15. He eats very slowly, and I waited for him for twenty minutes.

16. Is that matter which you told me about last week very important?

17. Please come in and sit down.

18. We will take you to the train station, ok?

19. Because the things he sells are too expensive, no one is willing to buy them.

20. I want to buy some stationery.

21. Who is that young lady?

22. 99,567

23. Don't get angry.

24. That matter isn't too important.

25. In the city there is a very large white house.

As an additional exercise, scan the above sentences and circle all characters which have simplified equivalents. Make sure you can write each of them.

LESSON XV

Ex. 17: Cross Character Puzzle. Complete the following just like a crossword puzzle.

Down
1. don't bring money along
2. older brother helps me do this
3. patients should not play

Across
1. don't cry
4. eldest brother is sick
5. I think it's not enough
6. unwilling to do
7. like that one

Ex. 18: Rewrite the following sentences, replacing simplified characters with full characters and vice versa.

1. 你愿意帮你的朋友吗？
2. 他很喜歡帶小孩子出去玩兒。
3. 朋友家里有事，我觉得我应当去帮他们一点儿忙。
4. 我不願意幫他買書。
5. 他带了两万块钱，应当够了。

THE CHARACTER BOOK: REVIEW LESSON C

(Lessons 11-15)

Exercises

Ex. 1: Name the part of speech that all of the following characters belong to, and give two examples of the use of each character in a phrase.

張　個　分　句　塊　些　位　件

Ex. 2: Make a combination (expression) for each of the following characters. Translate the expressions you make into English.

哥	_____	報	_____
開	_____	校	_____
訴	_____	夫	_____
定	_____	夜	_____
怎	_____	見	_____
放	_____	氣	_____
平	_____	孩	_____
喜	_____	棹	_____
幫	_____	玩	_____
認	_____	教	_____

Ex. 3: Write the Yale romanization for the following.

唱歌 _____   緊張 _____

已經 _____   打算 _____

怎麼 _____   願意 _____

吃過了 _____   哥哥 _____

忘了 _____   走路 _____

認識 _____   三刻鐘 _____

自己 _____   笑着 _____

火車 _____   找到了 _____

在街上 _____   大城 _____

工夫 _____   不懂 _____

REVIEW LESSON C

Ex. 4:   Translate into Chinese. (simplified characters)

1. Do you recognize that very tall man over there?

2. He went to school last night at midnight.

3. They have already run out.

4. Please put the desk on the road.

5. Because he forgot to buy vegetables, his wife is very angry.

6. My elder brother brought his children with him.

7. Which newspaper do you like to read?

8. He himself went to the city to help the sick man.

9. That little boy is only three years old, but he is very tall.

10. He smilingly said, "I can't find my teacher."

After completion, circle all simplified characters. Make sure you can write the regular form.

Ex. 5: Write the English equivalent beside the Chinese item.

哭 _____ 睡 _____ 應當 _____ 難 _____ 正在 _____

呢 _____ 底 _____ 生氣 _____ 茶 _____ 一分錢 _____

告訴 _____ 放在 _____ 教書 _____ 弟弟 _____ 水 _____

帶 _____ 忘 _____ 已經 _____ 玩 _____ 高 _____

Ex. 6: Translate the following phrases into Chinese and use each one in a sentence.

1. that woman who teaches school

2. this very tall girl

3. those very important affairs

4. those five sentences

5. tea that is good to drink

6. that person who is very willing to help

7. the children who don't understand Japanese

8. that teacher who is very angry

9. the people whom I don't recognize

10. the old woman who is reading the newspaper

REVIEW LESSON C

Ex. 7: Answer the following questions in Chinese. Your answers need not be truthful, but they must be grammatical and relevant to the questions.

1. 你三弟幾歲了?
2. 學中國話以後你打算作甚麼?
3. 你有幾個弟弟?哥哥呢?
4. 你現在有工夫沒有?
5. 誰不喜歡吃中國飯?
6. 你喜歡 hē 茶還是 hē 水?
7. 誰跟你一塊兒來?
8. 教中國話的那位先生是不是你哥哥?
9. 那個孩子為甚麼哭?
10. 你們已經來了幾天了?

Ex. 8:   Write the Chinese equivalents beside the English
         expressions.

school_____ tea_____ table_____ important_____

oneself_____ sing (songs)_____ Mrs. Jāng _____

see_____ stand up_____ how_____ already_____ almost_____

must_____ cross_____ should_____ enough_____ tell____

recognize_____ free time _____ look for_____ road____

white_____ street_____ thank you_____

Ex. 9:   Snaking its way through the jumble of characters
         in the box on the next page is the Chinese for
         "My older brother is sick. He can not sing, nor
         can he help me write letters. I am very angry
         because I must write to my girlfriend by myself;
         but I don't know how to write a letter." These
         are joined together without punctuation in the
         shape of the Chinese character for "middle"

REVIEW LESSON C

平	我	想	他	應	當	信	願	意	哭	帶	我	去
常	哥	昨	天	姓	張	寫	父	爲	甚	麼	還	玩
我	哥	今	天	明	天	麼	母	百	朋	友	幾	半
認	喜	所	以	念	書	怎	親	高	緊	就	會	聽
識	歡	氣	道	門	鐘	道	家	見	一	吧	是	走
他	生	生	知	出	起	知	塊	不	定	呢	可	寫
笑	病	很	從	把	等	不	早	必	跟	怎	友	字
底	信	我	很	生	氣	因	我	是	可	友	朋	日
睡	寫	太	太	老	位	爲	點	叫	告	訴	女	四
放	我	又	快	又	慢	我	歲	歌	夜	弟	的	貴
工	幫	再	著	子	孩	得	唱	懂	忘	城	我	大
夫	能	不	也	歌	唱	能	自	已	寫	信	給	得
打	送	行	情	事	件	不	站	男	女	新	眞	我
算	已	經	差	不	多	他	天	我	禮	拜	進	爲
上	校	白	天	晚	上	了	白	思	自	拿	愛	因
街	學	少	多	不	火	病	筆	誰	房	已	你	們
買	教	刻	開	關	水	哥	紙	的	子	我	寫	他
菜	分	來	過	得	跑	哥	信	表	手	萬	千	信
賣	茶	自	已	寫	信	我	哥	哥	病	了	他	不

"My older brother is sick. He can not sing, nor can he help me write letters. I am very angry because I must write to my girlfriend by myself; but I don't know how to write a letter." These are joined together without punctuation in the shape of the Chinese character for "middle"

Ex. 10: Cross Character Puzzle. Complete the following just like a crossword puzzle.

Down
1. How old is he this year?
2. Three and one half years
3. railway (or bus) station
4. He did not come the night before yesterday.
5. Whom are you looking for?
6. I don't like to cook.
7. five books
8. have eaten before

Across
2. third younger brother
4. year before last
9. train
10. He came to look for me last night at midnight.
11. Who doesn't understand?
12. last Friday
13. did not eat
14. to work
15. have been here already
16. lunch

REVIEW LESSON C

Ex. 11: What/who are you? Find the answer to this question by solving the key sentence in the boxes below. You fill in the boxes by completing the sentences below, or answering the questions posed in these sentences. One example is done for you. Place your answers in the boxes, which should give your identification in the vertical column of boxes.

1. ____，你們，他們

2. 你 ____ 誰？

3. 你現在在哪國？

4. 你學甚麼話？

5. 學生念書的地方

6. 教書的人

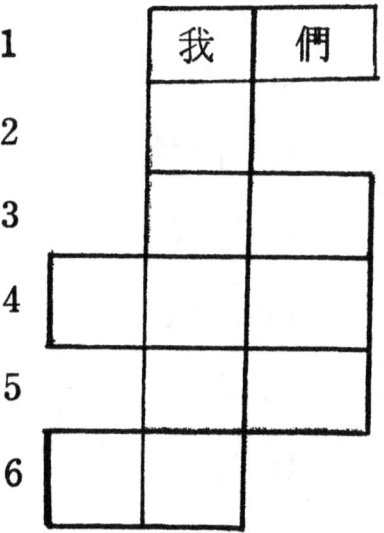

Ex. 12: Match the expressions in column A with their opposites in column B. One example is given.

A	B
1. 哥哥	a 在家
2. 先生	b 火
3. 上街	c 哭
4. 前	d 夜裏
5. 開	e 慢
6. 男	f 外頭
7. 笑	g 後
8. 水	h 去
9. 快	i 弟弟
10. 來	j 學生
11. 自己	k 母
12. 白天	l 關
13. 裏頭	m 女
14. 父	n 賣
15. 買	o 別人

Ex. 13: Rewrite the following sentences, replacing simplified characters with full characters and vice versa.

1. 我对他说:"谢谢你帮我母亲的忙。"
2. 你認識錢先生嗎?
3. 谁愿意带小孩出去玩儿?
4. 你不应当把钟给张先生。
5. 那個賣報的去過火車站沒有?
6. 他告诉我他现在已经四十岁了。

THE CHARACTER BOOK
LESSON XVI

A. Exercises on Character Meaning and Use

Ex. 1: Draw lines connecting the Chinese and English equivalents.

辦事　　　　　easy
法文　　　　　store (simplified)
怕　　　　　　store (regular)
办　　　　　　be broken
容易　　　　　manage (simplified)
客人　　　　　manage (regular)
错　　　　　　fear that
衣 shang　　　U.S.A.
壞了　　　　　bad person
法子　　　　　Chinese language
不錯　　　　　method
完了　　　　　clothes
睡覺　　　　　not bad
鋪子　　　　　be wrong
辦　　　　　　feel
覺得　　　　　finished
坏人　　　　　guest
美國　　　　　French
中文　　　　　sleep
铺子　　　　　handle a matter

LESSON XVI

Ex. 2: Write the letter of the English equivalent beside the Chinese items.

___ 壞人	___ 客人	___ 辦事	___ 日文
___ 有名	___ 不錯	___ 鋪子	___ 覺得
___ 唱完	___ 客氣	___ 容易	___ 怕太太
___ 美國	___ 錯了	___ 衣 shang	

a. easy
b. shop
c. feel
d. guest
e. clothes
f. famous
g. America
h. be wrong
i. hen-pecked
j. finished singing
k. bad person
l. handle the matter
m. Japanese language
n. be polite
o. not bad

Ex. 3: Write the English equivalents beside the Chinese items.

怕 ___	容易 ___	壞 ___	錯了 ___
鋪子 ___	美國 ___	法子 ___	有客 ___
壞人 ___	辦事 ___	完了 ___	覺得 ___
中文 ___	有名 ___	怎麼辦？ ___	
鋪子裡 ___	現在 ___	客气 ___	觉得 ___

Ex. 4:   Write the Chinese equivalents beside the English items.

be afraid to see people_____   easy_____

broken_____ guest_____ feel_____ America_____

can't be finished_____ not bad_____ store_____

Chinese language_____ famous_____ France_____

clothes_____ polite_____ handle the matter_____

sleep_____ cannot feel it_____ fear that_____

bad person (simplified)_____

what can be done about it (simp.)_____

LESSON XVI

Ex. 5:   Translate the following into English.

1. 這本書很不容易懂。
2. 先生說:「不對！你說錯了。」
3. 那個鋪子賣甚麼東西？
4. 高先生說他怕太太，高太太說他怕先生。
5. 他昨天夜裏睡不着覺。
6. 美國人喜歡吃中國菜嗎？
7. <u>張美一</u>不太客氣，可是他很會辦事。
8. 法文難還是中文難？
9. 有名的人都很會說話嗎？
10. 那些小孩子甚麼時候唱完？

Ex. 6: Complete the following sentences using (among others) characters from lesson 16.

1. 他的中文不太好。他常常 _____
2. 請高有用給我 _____
3. 他打算作買賣 _____
4. 他那個手表不能用．昨 _____
5. 有一個中國人 _____
6. 有一個意大 lì (Italy) 人 _____
7. 他昨天晚上請了七個人到他家去，可是 _____
8. 我不認識他，可是 _____
9. 我在大學念 _____
10. 他說很難作，可是我說 _____

LESSON XVI   231

Ex. 7:   Translate into Chinese. Note that in these items
          there are parts which are obligatory in English
          which do not occur in Chinese sentences.

1. It is easy to do.

2. It is very difficult to write.

3. It is finished.

4. It was a little bit wrong.

5. It got broken.

6. What can be done about it?

7. There is no way (to help it).

8. There is not enough tea.

9. There are not enough dishes.

10. It is not very easy to do.

Ex. 8:   Translate into Chinese.

1. Chinese is not very hard to study.

2. He is very famous, but I don't know him.

3. When they had finished singing, the teacher said, "Not bad, not bad."

4. That shop sells very good Chinese tea.

5. Jang Mei-yi can handle the matter.

6. People say that hen-pecked men are very wealthy.

7. Mr. Wang is really too polite.

8. In France, many people speak Chinese.

9. How did the big clock get broken?

10. Those clothes aren't very good looking.

LESSON XVI

Ex. 9:   Translate into Chinese. (write simplified characters)

1. That man wearing French clothes is a friend of mine.

2. That old man who is afraid of his wife is French.

3. This book that is easy to read is in Chinese.

4. That broken watch is now at school.

5. Who is that famous woman?

6. That very polite old gentleman used to teach Chinese.

7. The children who were playing there came over.

8. That man who likes to talk too much really should leave.

9. The school on the highway is terribly small.

10. The little girl who is good looking was playing with them this morning.

B. Exercises on the Story

Ex. 10: Answer the following questions on the story.

1. 那個美國人在中國作甚麼？
2. 他的中文好不好？
3. 誰到他家去看他？
4. 那個人爲甚麼很快就走了。
5. 那個美國人爲甚麼說不 gānjing？
6. 後來有一個中國人對他說甚麼？
7. 哪三句話差不多在甚麼地方都能用？
8. 那個美國人爲甚麼覺得那三句話很有用？
9. 那個美國人知道不知道甚麼時候說甚麼話？
10. 你覺得這三句話眞有用麼？

LESSON XVI

Ex. 11: The following is an English version of the first two paragraphs of the story. Translate them back into Chinese, and compare your translation with the original.

There was an American who taught English in China. His English wasn't bad, but his Chinese wasn't too good. There were a lot of things (speech) he didn't understand. And there were a lot of things that he said incorrectly. He often said, "English is very easy. Chinese is very difficult."

There was once a very famous Chinese person who went to his house to visit him. That person just came into the living room, (and) he wanted to say in Chinese, "Please sit down," but he said it wrongly. He said, "Please leave, please leave." That person heard this remark and left.

Ex. 12:   CONTROLLED COMPOSITION. Write one paragraph about a Frenchman living in the U.S. and having trouble with his English. When he speaks French, people don't understand, but they smile. When he speaks English, they don't understand, but they don't smile either. He also doesn't understand English when spoken by Americans. Because he learned English in France, he can speak English very well with French people, and when he returns to France he tells his English teacher there how badly the Americans speak English.

Ex. 13:   CONTROLLED COMPOSITION. Write a paragraph about your first week in Peking. You have been told that the three expressions 不錯，對了，沒法子 can be used anywhere, and you use them in contexts where it is embarrassing.

LESSON XVI

C. Exercise on Character Origin and Shape

Ex. 14: Write the characters from Lesson 16 with the following components.

宀：

口：

亠：

金：

D. Review Exercises

Ex. 15: Translate the following sentences into Chinese.

1. A famous French guest is coming to this store.
2. I feel that all Chinese schools are well managed.
3. There are many famous places in the U.S.A.
4. Chinese is really not easy.
5. I am not afraid of bad persons.
6. She couldn't sleep last night.
7. What can be done about it?
8. Do you have French books?
9. He is very polite.
10. His Japanese is not bad.

Ex. 16.: SEEK AND FIND. Circle and write out the Chinese equivalents of the expressions listed below.

事	衣	鋪	文	中	人	覺	認
客	辦	客	了	壞	法	名	得
文	容	完	容	文	國	美	中
名	錯	辦	人	日	書	衣	國
法	名	有	客	太	衣	太	太
怕	易	覺	法	氣	太	美	錯
完	壞	子	易	衣	辦	怕	眞
辦	生	眞	中	容	美	子	容
客	氣	文	國	見	易	睡	壞
覺	不	了	文	人	覺	子	易
美	錯	車	麼	唱	美	完	鋪

1. guest
2. famous
3. method
4. be polite
5. Chinese language
6. hen-pecked
7. finished
8. handle the matter
9. sleep
10. U.S.A.
11. easy
12. not wrong
13. shop
14. bad person
15. feel

LESSON XVI

Ex. 17: Rewrite the following sentences, replacing simplified characters with full characters and vice versa.

1. 请问这个书铺卖法国书吗？
2. 我覺得那個美國學校辦得不錯。
3. 这个事情不容易办，错一点儿，就坏了。
4. 那個鋪子裏頭的美國表不壞。
5. 我睡觉的时候不喜欢有人说话。

THE CHARACTER BOOK
LESSON XVII

A. Exercises on Character Meaning and Use

Ex. 1: Draw lines connecting the Chinese and English equivalents.

船	the most, -est
鱼	this road
最	black
次	occasion (measure word)
黑	mountain
画儿	extremely expensive
長	river
更	fish (simplified)
这条路	still more, even more
比一比	long
一樣	fish (regular)
河	painting (simplified)
難極了	painting (regular)
魚	short
样子	compare (them)
短	same
那條街	that street
畫兒	exceedingly difficult
山	style, appearance
贵极了	boat

240

LESSON XVII

Ex. 2: Write the letter of the English equivalent beside the Chinese items.

___ 樣子 ___ 大河 ___ 畫畫兒 ___ 船上

___ 最好 ___ 黑 ___ 山 ___ 沒法子比

___ 下次 ___ 長極了 ___ 天黑了 ___ 短

___ 更好 ___ 最晚 ___ 短好些

a. style
b. next time
c. incomparable
d. it would be best
e. even better
f. extremely long
g. short
h. paint a picture

i. big river
j. on the boat
k. the day has darkened
l. at the latest
m. a good deal shorter
n. black
o. mountain

Ex. 3: Write the English equivalent beside the Chinese items.

這條路 _____ 上次 _____ 比他大 _____

太長 _____ 更短 _____ 最高 _____

怎麼樣 _____ 黑紙 _____ 畫中國畫 _____

小魚 _____ 這次 _____ 船 _____

河裏 _____ 山上 _____ 那條？_____

這樣子 _____ 黑人 _____ 一樣 _____

为什么 _____ 願意 _____ 一点儿 _____

Ex. 4: Write the Chinese equivalent beside the English items.

black clothes_____ taller than I_____ long_____

short_____ how about?_____ paint_____ river_____

once upon a time_____ most interesting_____

fish_____ style, appearance_____ even better_____

this road_____ one river_____ at the latest_____

extremely expensive_____ painting (simp.)_____

same (simp.)_____ exceedingly difficult (simp.)_____

_____

Ex. 5: Translate the following phrases into English.

1. on the mountain   6. in that river

2. in the river   7. behind that house

3. in the boat   8. in front of that painting

4. on the table   9. outside the school

5. under the table   10. under the painting

LESSON XVII   243

Ex. 6:   Translate the following phrases into Chinese.

1. the long one   6. these three long rivers

2. this very short one   7. these large pictures

3. those very small ones   8. three small fish

4. these tall ones   9. that little boat

5. those long fish   10. the longest river

Ex. 7:   Translate the following phrases into Chinese.

1. very tall   6. too short

2. the tallest one   7. the most important

3. very short   8. too expensive

4. the shortest one   9. the most good looking one

5. extremely long   10. even uglier

Ex. 8: Translate the following phrases into English.

1. faster than a boat

2. taller than I

3. slower than a train

4. shorter than that one

5. longer than that one

6. more important than this

7. shorter than those fish

8. higher than that mountain

9. longer than this river

10. older than Mr. Jāng

LESSON XVII

Ex. 9: Translate into Chinese (simplified characters).

1. There is a beautiful woman on the mountain path.

2. The painting he painted was too dark.

3. He said last time that he wouldn't write the letter for me.

4. What is the longest river in China?

5. The shortest is the best.

6. That boat is even longer than this one.

7. The fish that he sells are extremely expensive.

8. These two are the same.

9. That black book and this one aren't alike.

10. Which street does he live on?

Ex. 10: Translate the following sentences into English.

1. 他買了那所黑房子嗎？
2. 哪條河長？是這條，還是那條？
3. 今天是星期六，我想上山。
4. 你那條魚不好吃，你最好吃這條。
5. 他對我說：「怎麼樣」，可是我沒聽懂。
6. 他那條船很好看，可是我這條更好看。
7. 中國畫兒我都喜歡看。
8. 高太太比高先生老嗎？
9. 他們賣的東西貴極了，你最好去別的鋪子買。
10. 哪個好？請你比一比。

LESSON XVII

Ex. 11: Complete the following sentences using (among others) characters from lesson 17.

1. 哪條短？ _____
2. 這本書我_____
3. 他跑得快，可是他哥哥_____
4. 中國人請客的時候，一定吃_____
5. 他怎麼來？_____
6. 畫上的_____
7. 張太太甚麼時候說的？他_____
8. 他的房子小，可是_____
9. 他眞的錢不够，他_____
10. 這條河比_____

B. Exercises on the Story

Ex. 12: Answer the following questions on the story.

1. 我們看見畫兒的時候常愛說甚麼？
2. 我們看見好看的地方的時候，常愛說甚麼？
3. 書上說是畫的比眞的好，還是眞的比畫的好？
4. 「山水畫兒」Yīng文怎麼說？
5. 那張山水畫兒上有甚麼？
6. 畫上的山，河都怎麼樣？
7. 我看了好看的畫，就想：＿＿＿＿＿＿＿＿＿＿
8. 後來我到哪兒去了？
9. 眞的山水怎麼樣？
10. 我看了一張很有名的畫兒，畫兒上有甚麼東西？
11. 我有一位朋友說甚麼？
12. 那張畫兒爲甚麼有名？
13. 爲甚麼人人都喜歡那張畫兒？
14. 最後「我」覺得眞的好還是畫的好？
15. 你喜歡不喜歡看畫兒？

LESSON XVII 249

Ex. 13: Below is an English version of paragraph two of the story. Translate it back into Chinese, and compare your translation with the original.

Once I saw a landscape painting. What was painted was a very famous river in China. In (on) that painting, the mountains were very tall, the river was very long, truly it was extremely good looking. When I looked at the lovely painting, I then thought: if one went to the real place, certainly the real place would be better than the painting. Afterwards, one year, I really went to that place. Looking from the mountain top, that river was very short, and I felt the place was very ordinary, not as good looking as the painting. I thought: What is painted is better than what is real.

Ex. 14: CONTROLLED COMPOSITION. Write a brief composition about your love of reading stories. You love to read stories. You especially love to read stories about people who live in (on) the mountains, and you love reading about long rivers, high mountains, and lovely places. But if you go to those places, you always find that the mountains are shorter than in the story, and the rivers are shorter. So you feel that stories are better than reality.

Ex. 15: CONTROLLED COMPOSITION. Write a paragraph or two about your painting. You love to paint. You like to paint landscapes. You especially like to paint rivers and mountains. In your rivers there are big fish. On your mountains are tiny houses. On your rivers are large boats, and in the boats are handsome people. Unfortunately, when people look at your pictures, they always ask, "What is that?" They do not recognize your mountains, rivers, houses, fish, and people for what they are.

C. Review Exercises

Ex. 16: Write the Chinese equivalents beside the English items.

100_____ person_____ large_____ small_____

I_____ you_____ recognize_____ free time_____ play_____

street_____ help_____ enough_____ what_____

place_____ eat rice_____ parents_____ mother_____

fast_____ exit_____ don't_____ meaning_____ see_____

OK or not?_____ week_____ love_____ because_____

urgent_____ hear_____ almost_____ stand up_____

forget_____ hard_____ newspaper_____ fire_____

water_____ school_____

LESSON XVII   251

Ex. 17:   Translate the following into Chinese.

1. Why haven't you closed the door yet?

2. What time does your school start (open) next year?

3. They plan on going to China year after next.

4. His older brother got sick yesterday, and is sleeping today.

5. I feel that the people in that store aren't too polite.

6. Writing Chinese characters is easy; painting Chinese pictures is not easy.

7. Have you finished singing yet?

8. How many books did you buy last night?

9. Please tell me how to say "Help, I want to get out of here!" in Chinese.

10. The white paper is pretty, but the black paper is even prettier.

Ex. 18: Rewrite the following sentences, replacing simplified characters with full characters and vice versa.

1. 你觉得画鱼难，还是画河难？
2. 他畫的這條魚長極了。
3. 这个样子的山比那个样子的山更好看。
4. 我們今天晚飯吃魚，怎麼樣？
5. 这张画里头的那条鱼画得好极了。

LESSON XVII

Ex. 19: CROSS CHARACTER PUZZLE. Complete the following just like a crossword puzzle.

Down
1. to paint a picture
2. on the boat
3. the day has darkened
4. mountain path
5. a big river
6. long is better than short
7. sell fish

Across
8. ride on a boat
9. daytime
10. painting
11. go up a mountain
12. the road is extremely long
13. a boat
14. The fish is in the river.
15. extremely good

THE CHARACTER BOOK
LESSON XVIII

A. Exercises on Character Meaning and Use

Ex. 1: Draw lines connecting the Chinese and English equivalents.

飯館兒	far (simplified)
酒	restaurant (simplified)
穿	near
边	straight on
南	leave, separate
左	restaurant (regular)
幫忙	help (somebody)
遠	far (regular)
旧	drink
近	busy
一直	old (in use) (simplified)
喝	north
远	left
忙	side (simplified)
北	side (regular)
邊兒	right
饭馆儿	south
右	wear
舊	old (in use) (regular)
離開	liquor

LESSON XVIII

Ex. 2: Put the letter of the English equivalent in the blank beside the appropriate Chinese expression.

穿衣	_____	a. become old
離這兒遠	_____	b. go straight on
離開	_____	c. leave, separate
賣酒的	_____	d. tea house
舊了	_____	e. wine seller
一直走	_____	f. left hand
忙不忙	_____	g. front (side)
近多了	_____	h. southwest
喝酒	_____	i. quite far from here
多遠？	_____	j. drink liquor
西南	_____	k. busy or not?
前邊兒	_____	l. much nearer
左手	_____	m. how far?
茶館兒	_____	n. put on clothes
東北	_____	o. northeast

Ex. 3: In the blanks, write the English equivalents of the following Chinese expressions.

邊 _____ 右 _____ 離 _____ 喝 _____ 穿 _____

忙 _____ 舊 _____ 近 _____ 左 _____ 北 _____

南 _____ 一直走 _____ 茶館兒 _____

遠 _____ 離開 _____ 不好 _____

幫忙 _____ 下邊兒 _____

Ex. 4: In the blanks, write the Chinese equivalents of the following English expressions.

southeast _____ the left side _____ how far? _____

go straight on _____ restaurant _____ northwest _____

displeasing to the taste (drinking) _____

unable to put on (clothes) _____

help (somebody) _____ old things _____ wine seller _____

not too near _____ right side _____ the top _____

leave, separate _____ which side? (simp.) _____

quite far from here (simp.) _____ restaurant (simp.) _____

LESSON XVIII

Ex. 5: Translate the following phrases into Chinese.

1. on the right side

2. on the left side

3. on the top (side)

4. on the bottom (below)

5. on the west side

Ex. 6: Translate the following phrases into Chinese.

1. very far

2. very close

3. very far from here

4. very close to here

5. not far from here

6. on the west

7. go straight on

8. in the front

9. on the east side

10. on the back

Ex. 7: Complete each of the following sentences by inserting place expressions. One example is given.

Example: 學校在 <u>前邊兒</u>，<u>離</u>這兒<u>不遠</u>。

1. 他們家 _____
2. 我們現在在 _____ 玩。
3. 小孩子們 _____ 念書
4. 學校 _____ 他們家 _____
5. 日本 _____ 中國的 _____
6. 先生問我酒館兒有多遠，我說：「____這兒____。」
7. 「書桌在哪兒？」「_____。」
8. _____ 有很多中國書。
9. 先生 _____ 館兒的 _____ 睡着了。
10. 那個飯館兒 _____ 還是 _____？

LESSON XVIII   259

Ex. 8:   Complete the following sentences using (among others) characters from lesson 18.

1. 我哥哥在路 _____
2. 他很喜歡幫 _____
3. 左邊兒 _____
4. 車站離這兒 _____
5. 我問老人怎麼走，他 _____
6. 那位日本人賣的東西都 _____
7. _____ 新衣。
8. _____ 手寫字。
9. 我請他 _____ 他說他不能 _____
10. 因為他們的事情 _____

Ex. 9:   Translate the following into English.

1. 我母親不要我喝酒，可是他走了以後我就到酒館兒去了。
2. 學校離這兒很近，比車站近多了。
3. 我先看北邊，然後看南邊，最後看西邊。
4. 右邊有一個北方人，左邊有一個南方人，你怕哪個？
5. 我穿好看的衣 shang 到飯館兒去吃飯。
6. <u>張文一</u>常常很忙，可是很願意幫別人的忙。
7. 右手不知道左手在作甚麼。
8. 小孩子問父母：「遠東有多遠？」
9. 小孩子問父母：「是舊東西好還是新東西好？」
10. 這個地方好看，東南西北都有山，都有水。

LESSON XVIII

Ex. 10: Translate the following into Chinese.

1. Is the tea house farther or the restaurant farther?

2. This American wine is displeasing to the taste.

3. American southerners wear pretty clothes.

4. Chinese northerners are all tall.

5. To get to the wine house, you have to go straight ahead.

6. The school is very close to here, but the tea house is very far.

7. He is very busy with his affairs, but he still likes to go out to eat Chinese food.

8. Right hand or left hand--which do you write with?

9. How do you say, "north, south, east, west," in Chinese?

10. Yesterday, he helped me at school.

B. Exercises on the Story

Ex. 11: Answer the following questions on the story.

1. 有一天我到哪兒去了？
2. 那個地方，我去過沒有？
3. 我是在哪兒吃的晚飯？
4. 我認識到火車站的路嗎？
5. 我在街上看見了一個甚麼樣的人？
6. 他穿的是甚麼樣的衣 shang ？
7. 他在街上走得怎麼樣？
8. 我過去問他甚麼？
9. 他說火車站遠不遠？
10. 他說到火車站怎麼走？

LESSON XVIII   263

Ex. 12:   CONTROLLED COMPOSITION. Write a paragraph about
          getting lost in a big city and meeting a man who
          has drunk too much. He asks you how to get home
          (i.e., how to get to his home). You say you
          don't know. He gets angry and asks you again.
          Because you don't want him to be angry, you give
          him some directions. He repeats the directions
          after you, but he gets everything backwards.

Ex. 13:   CONTROLLED COMPOSITION.

One day you go into a large city to visit a friend. You
knew his address was 124 High Street (高街一百二十四 hàu)
but you don't know where High Street is located. You meet
a small girl and ask her where High Street is, and she says
it is up on the sky. Then you meet an old man and he says
it is on the mountain tops. Finally you run into the friend
that you were going to visit. He is laughing. He asks
you why you have been on High Street in front of his house
for so long talking to people and not coming in.

C. Review Exercises

Ex. 14: Translate into Chinese.

1. Which river is the Black River--the one on the south side or the one on the north side?

2. The Black River is much longer than the White River, but the Great River is even longer.

3. The guests all said that store's things were excellent.

4. Which is larger, America or China?

5. Studying Chinese is much easier than studying English.

6. I don't know why that child likes to cry so much when we're playing.

7. You really shouldn't drink so much booze.

8. You're going to the north to study. I'm afraid you don't wear enough clothing.

9. I thanked him for helping me carry the huge clock.

10. There are a lot of very expensive houses on North Street.

11. But the houses on South Fifth Street are prettier.

LESSON XVIII 265

Ex. 14: (continued)

12. The wine house on the left has more wine than the one on the right.

13. Please put those things down on the right side of the house.

14. The clothes sold in that store are all too old. I won't buy or wear them.

15. He felt that American automobiles were too big.

16. The painter liked to paint the South Mountain very much.

17. My daughter cried at 1:30 last night.

18. If their house is so far from here, why must he walk? Why not go by car?

19. The fish are all spoiled. What can we do about it?

20. French people and American people both feel that Chinese is very easy to learn.

After completing this exercise, scan the twenty sentences circling any character having a simplified equivalent. Make certain you can write each of them.

Ex. 15: Write out the following romanized sentences in two ways: first in simplified characters and then in unsimplified characters.

1. Lǎu Jāng shwō fàngwǎn dzai jeityáu hé de běibyār.

2. Chǐngwèn, nèige Jūnggwo fàngwǎn lǐ sywésyàu ywǎn buywǎn.

3. Jwōdzshangbian yǒu lyǎngběn jiù shū.

4. Nèige pùdz de syīn shū hěn gùi.

5. Tā neityau yú chángjíle. Bǐ shéide dōu cháng.

THE CHARACTER BOOK
LESSON XIX

A. Exercises on Character Meaning and Use

Ex. 1: Draw lines connecting the Chinese and English equivalents.

奇怪　　　　　　king
毛　　　　　　　heart
脸　　　　　　　strange
往　　　　　　　maybe (simplified)
才　　　　　　　maybe (regular)
一毛錢　　　　　everyday
　　　　　　　　body hair
王　　　　　　　age (simplified)
也許　　　　　　age (regular)
臉　　　　　　　convenient
歲數　　　　　　to, towards
但　　　　　　　not until
方便　　　　　　wash
每天　　　　　　face (simplified)
心　　　　　　　face (regular)
要不然　　　　　10¢
洗　　　　　　　but
也许　　　　　　otherwise
歲數

267

Ex. 16: SEEK AND FIND. Locate, circle and write out the Chinese equivalents for the English items given below.

兒	南	一	忙	兒	邊	後	近
館	北	穿	直	館	不	北	忙
茶	左	舊	遠	太	喝	開	離
右	東	西	近	忙	邊	兒	西
西	喝	不	南	離	館	喝	酒
邊	好	的	舊	飯	上	左	離
喝	手	酒	忙	手	南	不	直
左	館	賣	幫	直	右	近	穿

1. southwest
2. left hand
3. the rear (side)
4. drink (liquor)
5. tea house
6. unable to put on (clothes)
7. help (somebody)
8. not too near
9. old things
10. leave, separate
11. straight on
12. wine seller
13. restaurant
14. displeasing to the taste (drinking)
15. right hand

LESSON XIX   269

Ex. 2:   Write the letter of the English equivalent beside
         the Chinese items.

___ 不但   ___ 洗臉   ___ 方便   ___ 五毛九

___ 要不然   ___ 歲數   ___ 奇怪   ___ 往東走

___ 姓王   ___ 才五點鐘   ___ 但   ___ 也許

___ 臉上   ___ 小心   ___ 每一個人

a. strange   i. surnamed Wang
b. if not, then   j. on the face
c. only 5:00   k. age
d. each person   l. convenient
e. not only   m. maybe
f. wash face   n. go towards the east
g. be careful   o. but
h. 59¢

Ex. 3:   Write the English equivalents beside the Chinese
         items.

點心 _____   王家 _____   眞奇怪 _____   但 _____

也許 _____   方便 _____   不但 _____   才三毛五 _____

歲數 _____   放心 _____   洗臉 _____   要不然 _____

便 _____   每張桌子 _____   姓王 _____

往西走 _____   每天 _____   洗一洗 _____

Ex. 4: Write the Chinese equivalents beside the English items.

strange_____ or else_____ just_____ not until_____

wash_____ heart_____ king_____ Mr. Wang_____ age_____

everyday_____ how strange_____ but_____otherwise_____

walk towards west_____ maybe_____ convenient_____

cheap_____ then and only then_____ face_____

10¢_____ rest assured_____ snacks_____

count money (simp.)_____ wash face (simp.)_____

not permitted to come (simp.)_____

Ex. 5: Translate into Chinese.

1. only 5:00

2. only 35¢

3. came just a moment ago

4. didn't leave until 3:00

5. won't go until tomorrow

6. only 6:45

7. only $4.00

8. didn't start school until 10 years old

9. couldn't come until last night

10. won't talk until you arrive

LESSON XIX

Ex. 6:   Translate into Chinese.

1. When Mr. Wang heard the foreigner speaking, he thought to himself (in his heart), "How strange!"

2. It is even more convenient to go by his car.

3. Go towards the west. Then you will certainly see the school.

4. There were snacks at each table.

5. If he is not singing Chinese songs, he is singing Japanese songs; otherwise he is singing German songs.

6. He got up, washed his face, and went to work.

7. Not only does he not wash his face, he does not wash his hands either.

8. This English book is very cheap, it only costs forty cents.

9. Do you know his age?

10. Mr. Wang said, "Be careful!"

B. Exercises on the Story

Ex. 7: Answer the following questions on the story.

1. 王先生名字叫甚麼？ 他兒子叫甚麼？
2. 國平作事作的得麼樣？
3. 「不是….就是」Ying 文怎麼說?
4. 你叫他念書，他也許說甚麼？
5. 他每天起來了就作甚麼？
6. 王老先生是誰？
7. 王老先生叫國平去買甚麼？
8. 國平問他甚麼？
9. 國平 gāng 走到門外就問甚麼?
10. 王老先生爲甚麼打國平？
11. 王老先生打了國平，國平就怎麼了?
12. 王老先生爲甚麼生氣？
13. 王思遠常打他兒子嗎？
14. 王思遠一聽他父親打了他兒子，他就作甚麼？
15. 王思遠爲甚麼打自已？

LESSON XIX 273

Ex. 8: The following sentences are translated from the story. Translate them back into Chinese, and check your translations against the original.

Wáng Gwópíng was ten years old, but he was very stupid and was careless when doing anything. If you asked him to do something for you, if he didn't forget it, then he wouldn't do it at all; otherwise he would do it wrong. If you told him to study, not only would he not study, but he would say, "what's the use of studying?"

Ex. 9: CONTROLLED COMPOSITION. Rewrite the last paragraph on p. 161. Change the names and sexes of the characters.

Ex. 10: CONTROLLED COMPOSITION. Write one paragraph about you trying to buy some wine but unable to find the wine shop. You ask for directions but you later find a restaurant instead of a wine shop, so you eat a dinner instead of buying wine.

C. Review Exercises

Ex. 11: Translate the following sentences into Chinese.

1. The things in that store are really cheap.

2. Not only does he wash his face once every morning; he also washes it once every night.

3. You'll know that he is not young by looking at his face.

4. If he is not working, he is writing characters; otherwise, he is reading books.

5. This book only costs 25¢.

6. He is always careless like this.

7. He goes out alone everyday.

8. Going by boat is not too convenient.

9. It only takes eighty cents by train.

10. Maybe it's only five o'clock.

LESSON XIX

Ex. 12: Rewrite the following sentences, replacing simplified characters with full characters, and vice versa.

1. 你看他的脸，就知道他岁数不小了。
2. 我小時候不喜歡洗臉。
3. 那个书铺也许有旧书。
4. 這兒的錢請你數一數。
5. 他的母亲不要他到酒馆儿去喝酒。

Ex. 13:   CROSS CHARACTER PUZZLE. Complete the following just like a crossword puzzle.

Down
1. I have fifty cents.
2. rest assured
3. His face has black spots.
4. wash hands
5. useful
6. really convenient

Across
2. put down
3. Maybe he has snacks.
4. wash face
7. no hair on the hand
8. place to spend money
9. did not come to Wang's family until six o'clock

THE CHARACTER BOOK: REVIEW LESSON D

(Lessons 1-19)

Exercises

Ex. 1: Write as many characters as you know to have one of the following components. One example is given.

a 言： 請，這，許，

b 亻

c 氵

d 口

e 女

f 宀

g 辶

h 竹

i 日

j 忄

k 心

l 門

m 木

n 土

o 金

Ex. 2: For the following expressions, give their opposites. One example is given.

1. 近 ⟶ _遠_
2. 新 ⟶ _____
3. 也許 ⟶ _____
4. 南 ⟶ _____
5. 左 ⟶ _____
6. 黑 ⟶ _____
7. 長 ⟶ _____
8. 哭 ⟶ _____
9. 開 ⟶ _____
10. 難 ⟶ _____
11. 白天 ⟶ _____
12. 女 ⟶ _____
13. 便yi ⟶ _____
14. 快 ⟶ _____
15. 西 ⟶ _____
16. 買 ⟶ _____
17. 多 ⟶ _____
18. 外 ⟶ _____
19. 前 ⟶ _____
20. 上 ⟶ _____

REVIEW LESSON D

Ex. 3: Use the following expressions to make sentences and also translate the sentences into English.

1. 要不然
2. 也許
3. 奇怪
4. 一直
5. 貴極了
6. 最要緊
7. 怎麼樣
8. 不容易
9. 覺得
10. 願意

Ex. 4: Translate the following sentences into Chinese.

1. Will going towards the west be all right?

2. Not only doesn't Mrs. Gāu wash her face, she doesn't wash her hands either.

3. Please be careful!

4. This wine is not good to drink.

5. There are people on both left and right.

6. This river is longer than that river.

7. That mountain is even higher.

8. The fish seller has two boats.

9. Can you teach me how to paint Chinese paintings?

10. American automobiles are not easily ruined.

REVIEW LESSON D

Ex. 5: Combine each of the characters in column A with each of those in column B to make phrases. Then add such characters as needed to make sentences.

```
    A  最            B  長
       更               短
       不               遠
       很               近
       多               忙
       眞               舊
```

Ex. 6: Write Yale romanizations for the following and also give their English equivalents.

1. 方便 _____   6. 西南 _____
2. 往東走 _____   7. 穿不上 _____
3. 歲數 _____   8. 右邊兒 _____
4. 洗臉 _____   9. 天黑了 _____
5. 離開 _____   10. 覺得 _____

Ex. 7: Translate the following phrases into Chinese and use each one in a sentence.

1. a very strange person

2. otherwise I'll go

3. not only

4. rest assured

5. help him

6. at the latest

7. even better

8. next time

9. not wrong

10. finished writing

Ex. 8: Answer the following questions in Chinese. Your answers need not be truthful, but they must be grammatical and relevant to the questions.

1. 中文容易還是法文容易？
2. 你的朋友裏有有名的人嗎？
3. 你常常晚上不睡覺嗎？
4. 是他怕他太太還是他太太怕他？
5. 船比河更大，對不對？
6. 你會畫畫兒嗎？
7. 甚麼事情最有意思？
8. 酒館離學校遠不遠？
9. 你每天洗臉嗎？
10. 姓王的歲數多大了？

Ex. 9: Write the Chinese equivalent beside the English expressions.

1. ten cents _____
2. snacks _____
3. how strange _____
4. tea house _____
5. help (some one) _____
6. southwest _____
7. the day has darkened _____
8. it would be best _____
9. even more important _____
10. taller than I _____
11. extremely long _____
12. this street _____
13. style _____
14. ride on a boat _____
15. in the river _____
16. mountain path _____
17. store _____
18. handle the matter _____
19. finished singing _____
20. be polite _____

Ex. 10: Can you name the things below by their descriptions? One example is given.

1. __船__ ：在河上走的，人可以坐在上頭的東西

2. _____ ：在河裏住的，可以吃的東西

3. _____ ：喝酒的地方

4. _____ ：賣東西的地方

5. _____ ：很多人每天晚上十二點鐘的時候作的事情

6. _____ ：他是你父母的兒子，他的歲數比你大，他是你的甚麼人？

7. _____ ：人可以在上頭走的東西

8. _____ ：中國人喜歡喝的東西（不是酒）

9. _____ ：房子裏的一個屋子，裏頭有很多書，可以在那兒念書

10. _____ ：要是你想知道現在是甚麼時候，你可以看那個東西（那個東西不在你的手上）

Ex. 11: SEEK AND FIND. Locate, circle, and write out the Chinese equivalent for the English items given below.

工	怪	賣	酒	易	病	的
應	酒	大	歲	美	當	人
的	奇	便	容	要	歲	應
也	子	方	洗	自	數	人
許	美	棹	火	己	車	易
子	人	不	怪	工	容	病
應	當	奇	車	夫	火	酒
棹	病	方	國	自	臉	車
當	臉	火	美	要	不	然
洗	奇	然	便	已	自	歲

1. strange
2. maybe
3. otherwise
4. convenient
5. wash face
6. age
7. wine seller
8. easy
9. U.S.A.
10. should
11. sick person
12. free time
13. self
14. table
15. train

Ex. 12: Figure out the key sentence in the crossword by completing the nine sentences below. The key sentence begins at 1 down. Two examples are given.
The last word of the key sentence may be new to you!

1. 那個跟 ____ ____.
2. 你 ____ 美國人吧！
3. 請你 ____ ____ 洗你的臉。
4. 離中國一個不遠的地方就是 ____ ____.
5. 中國有 ____ ____ 人
6. 他的女朋友很 ____ ____.
7. 這個東西是 ____ ____.
8. 你會寫 ____ ____ 嗎？
9. 學生都得 ____ ____ 、

Ex. 13: Draw lines connecting the simplified and the regular characters.

个 什 么 头 儿 后 东 卖 对 时 写 问 会 几 点 听 为 还 坏 办 边 万 书 过 关

關 書 麼 東 對 會 兒 賣 寫 幾 個 聽 壞 後 邊 爲 問 甚 頭 時 點 還 辦 萬 過

APPENDIX I
Stroke Order List For Simplified Characters in <u>Read Chinese I</u>

<u>Lesson One</u>

1. 个 ₃ ノ 人 个
2. 们 ₅ ノ 亻 仃 仃 们
3. 两 ₇ 一 丆 两 丙 丙 两 两

<u>Lesson Two</u>

1. 什 ₄ ノ 亻 仁 什
2. 么 ₃ ノ 厶 么
3. 吗 ₆ 丶 冂 口 叮 吗 吗
*4. 嗎 ₁₃ 丶 冂 口 口丶 口三 口丰 嗎 嗎 嗎 嗎 嗎
5. 里 ₇ 丶 冂 日 日 旦 甲 甲 里
6. 后 ₆ ノ 厂 厂 斤 后 后
7. 头 ₅ 丶 ㇒ 三 头 头
8. 这 ₇ 丶 亠 方 文 文 这 这
9. 儿 ₂ ノ 儿
10. 哪 ₉ 丶 冂 口 叮 叨 明 明 哪 哪

289

Lesson Three

1. 说 9 丶 讠 讠 讠 讠 讠 诌 诌 说
2. 话 8 丶 讠 讠 计 计 话 话 话
3. 国 8 丨 冂 冂 冃 团 囯 国 国
4. 来 7 一 一 ㄅ 五 乎 来 来
5. 给 9 ㄥ ㄠ 乡 纟 纠 纹 给 给 给

Lesson Four

1. 时 7 丨 冂 日 日 时 时 时
2. 钱 10 丿 𠂉 𠂉 钅 钅 钅 钅 钱 钱 钱
3. 东 5 一 ㄊ 车 车 东
4. 买 6 フ ˇ ˇ 买 买 买
5. 卖 8 一 十 十 十 士 壶 卖 卖
6. 对 5 フ 又 又 对 对

APPENDIX I

Lesson Five

1. 饭 ₇ ノ 𠂉 𠂊 𠂋 饣 饣 饭
2. 请 ₁₀ 丶 讠 讠 讠 讠 讠 请 请 请 请
3. 问 ₆ 丶 亠 门 问 问 问
4. 写 ₅ 丶 冖 冖 写 写
5. 学 ₈ 丶 丷 丷 丷 兴 学 学 学
6. 会 ₆ ノ 人 𠆢 会 会 会

Lesson Six

1. 儿 ₂ ノ 儿
2. 点 ₉ 丨 卜 上 占 占 点 点 点 点
3. 听 ₇ 丨 刀 口 口 听 听 听
4. 现 ₈ 一 二 干 王 𤣩 玑 现 现
5. 为 ₄ 丶 丿 为 为
6. 还 ₇ 一 丆 才 不 不 还 还

Lesson Seven

1. 亲 ₉ 、 亠 ㇊ 方 立 亍 亲 亲 亲
2. 块 ₇ 一 十 土 圠 坧 坬 块
3. 书 ₄ ㇇ 乛 书 书

Lesson Eight

1. 门 ₃ 、 冂 门
2. 钟 ₉ 丿 人 乍 卢 钅 钅 钅 钅 钟
3. 从 ₄ 丿 人 从 从

Lesson Nine

1. 爱 ₁₀ 丿 乀 爫 爫 爫 爫 爫 爫 爱 爱
2. 进 ₇ 一 二 キ 井 讲 讲 进
3. 贵 ₉ 、 冂 口 中 虫 早 贵 贵 贵

Lesson Ten

1. 纸 ₇ 乚 乡 乡 纟 纟 纸 纸
2. 笔 ₁₀ 丿 ㇒ 𠂉 𠂉 竹 竹 竺 竺 笔 笔
3. 谁 ₁₀ 、 讠 讠 计 讣 讣 讠 讠 谁 谁
4. 万 ₃ 一 丆 万

APPENDIX I

Lesson Eleven

1. 气 ₄ 丿 ⺅ ⺊ 气
2. 张 ₈ 丨 ⺋ 弓 引 引 弘 张 张
3. 见 ₄ 丨 冂 贝 见
4. 紧 ₁₀ 丨 刂 刂⺊ 収 坚 坚 竖 紧 紧

Lesson Twelve

1. 岁 ₆ 丨 ⺊ 山 屮 岁 岁
2. 诉 ₇ 丶 ⺀ 讠 讠 诉 诉 诉
3. 经 ₈ ㄥ 纟 纟 纟 纟 经 经 经
4. 难 ₁₀ ㇇ 又 ⺙ 对 对 邓 难 难 难 难

Lesson Thirteen

1. 车 ₄ 一 ⺈ 左 车
2. 报 ₇ 一 十 扌 扣 护 扔 报
3. 开 ₄ 一 二 开 开
4. 关 ₆ 丶 丷 丷 兰 关 关
5. 谢 ₁₂ 丶 讠 讠 讠 讠 讠 讠 讠 讠 谢 谢 谢
6. 过 ₆ 一 寸 寸 寸 过 过

Lesson Fourteen

1. 认₄ 丶 讠 讣 认
2. 识₇ 丶 讠 让 训 识 识 识

Lesson Fifteen

1. 帮₁₀ 丿 ⼆ 三 丰 邦 邦 邦 帮 帮
2. 带₉ 一 十 卄 卅 卅 带 带 带 带
3. 欢₆ 丿 又 火 ᄊ 欢 欢
4. 应₇ 丶 二 广 广 庁 应 应
5. 当₆ 丶 ⺌ 当 当 当 当
6. 愿₁₄ 一 厂 厂 厂 厈 厉 盾 原 原 原 愿 愿 愿

Lesson Sixteen

1. 办₄ 丁 力 办 办
2. 觉₉ 丶 ⺌ 尚 尚 堂 堂 觉 觉
3. 错₁₃ 丿 亻 ⺄ 钅 钅 钅 钅 钅 钅 钅 错 错
4. 铺₁₂ 丿 亻 ⺄ 钅 钅 钅 钅 铂 钼 铺 铺
5. 坏₇ 一 十 土 扩 坏 坏 坏

APPENDIX I

Lesson Seventeen

1. 画 8　一 厂 闩 甶 画 画 画
2. 鱼 8　′ ⺈ 𠂎 𭕄 鱼 鱼 鱼
3. 样 10　一 十 才 才 木 术 村 栏 栏 样
4. 条 7　′ 久 夂 冬 条 条
5. 长 5　丿 レ 卜 长 长
6. 极 8　一 十 才 木 杉 杉 极

Lesson Eighteen

1. 边 5　⺆ 力 ′力 边 边
2. 馆 11　′ ⺈ 乞 乞 𠂉 𠂊 馆 馆 馆 馆
3. 远 7　一 二 テ 元 元 远 远
4. 旧 5　丨 ⺁ 𠂆 旧 旧
5. 离 10　丶 亠 亠 文 立 立 产 离 离 离

Lesson Nineteen

1. 脸 11　丿 月 月 月 月 𦙶 𦙷 脸 脸 脸 脸
2. 数 13　丶 丶 ソ 丬 才 米 米 娄 娄 娄 数 数 数
3. 许 6　丶 讠 讠 许 许 许

www.ingramcontent.com/pod-product-compliance
Lightning Source LLC
Chambersburg PA
CBHW051207290426
44109CB00021B/2376